THE T-34 RUSSIAN BATTLE TANK

DR. MATTHEW HUGHES
&
DR. CHRIS MANN

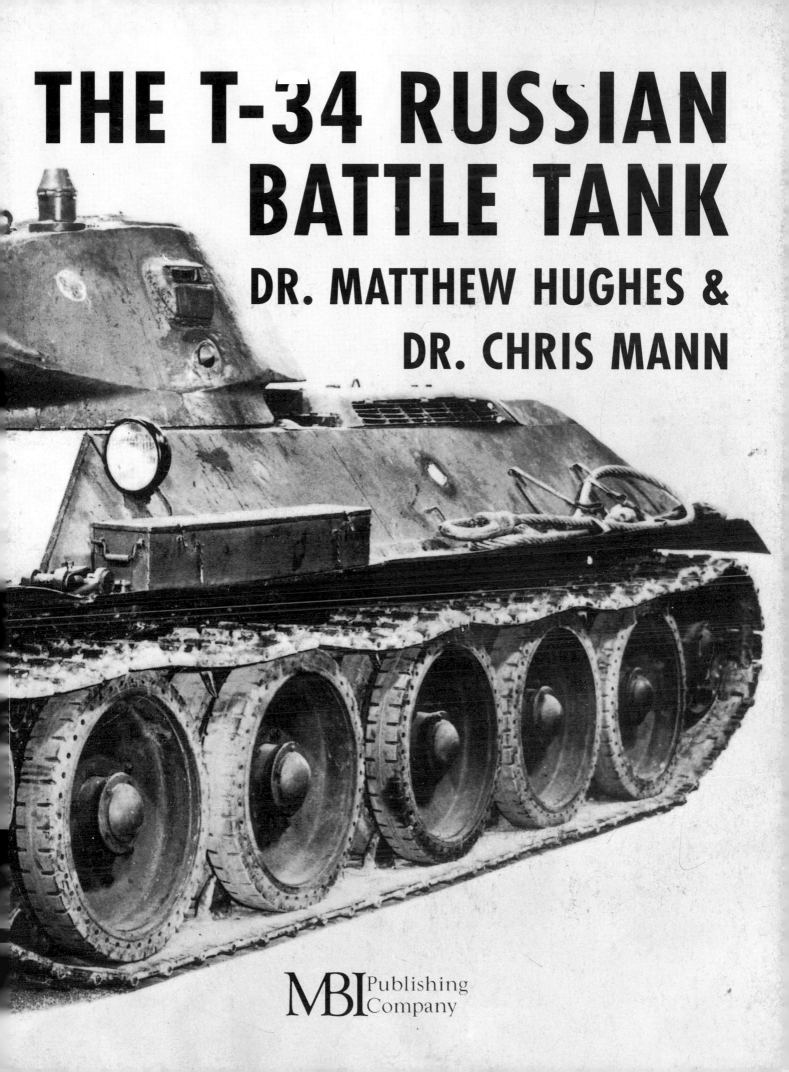

THE T-34 RUSSIAN BATTLE TANK

DR. MATTHEW HUGHES &
DR. CHRIS MANN

MBI Publishing Company

MBI Publishing Company books are also available at discounts in bulk quantity
for industrial or sales-promotional use. For details write to Special Sales Manager
at Motorbooks International Wholesalers & Distributors, 729 Prospect Avenue,
PO Box 1, Osceola, WI 54020-0001 USA.

Library of Congress Cataloging-in-Publication Data Available.

ISBN 0-7603-0701-6

Editorial and design: Amber Books Ltd
Bradley's Close, 74-77 White Lion Street,
London N1 9PF

Editor: Vanessa Unwin
Design: Keren Harrigan

Printed and bound in The Slovak Republic

Picture credits
Robert Hunt Library: 2-3, 54-55, 57, 68 (bottom), 70, 75, 80
John Norris: 89, 90
Tank Museum Collection, Bovington: 6-7, 11, 13, 14, 15, 16, 20, 21, 22, 23, 24, 26-27, 28, 29, 30, 34, 35, 36, 37, 38, 39, 40, 42, 43, 44, 45, 46, 47, 48-49, 50, 52, 53, 60, 61 (bottom), 64 (both), 65, 68 (top), 69, 72, 78, 82-83, 84, 85
TRH Pictures: 8, 9, 10, 12, 25, 56, 61 (top), 62, 73, 74, 76-77, 79, 81, 88, back cover

Artwork credits
Aerospace Publishing: 67 (bottom)
John Batchelor: 67 (top)
Bob Garwood: 32-33
Mainline Design: 18 (both), 19 (both), 66 (both), 86 (both), 87 (both)
Peter Sarson: 58-59

Pages 2-3: The T-34 medium tank – arguably the most important armored
fighting vehicle of World War II.

CONTENTS

CHAPTER 1

The Genesis of the T-34

Although the Soviet Union became interested in armoured warfare later than its European rivals, the Red Army made up for its late start by embracing mechanised war in the 1930s. This was nowhere more evident than in the development of the T-34 medium battle tank, arguably the best medium tank of World War II.

The T-34 tank was something special. Widely regarded as the most influential tank design of World War II, it was probably the best also. When it first saw combat in the summer of 1941, the T-34 was easily the most advanced tank in service. Tank design has always been a complex compromise between firepower, protection and mobility. Most tanks have had to sacrifice one or more of these factors in favour of the other, yet in the T-34 the Soviet designers achieved the perfect balance – no compromises had been made.

The 76.2mm gun had awesome hitting power by the standards of 1941, while the ground-breaking use of sloping armour gave superb protection. The tank's advanced diesel engine married to the Christie suspension system gave excellent cross-country performance. The invading Germans were awestruck.

The technical advantage did not last long, yet it is the mark of a superior weapon system, such as the T-34, that it could be easily adapted and upgraded. Unlike the Germans, the Soviets were not forced to design and build new vehicles and thus they avoided the delay and dislocation to production that would have entailed. A new, larger 85mm gun and heavier armour made the T-34 a formidable weapon once again. Indeed the T-34/85 makes the strongest claim of any of the T-34 family for the title of best all-round tank of any stage of the war. The design has also proved remarkably durable. It remained the Soviet main battle tank until the mid-1950s, and the Bosnian Serbs were still using T-34/85s during the

Left: A pristine, factory fresh T-34 Model 1942. This trial sample was sent to the United Kingdom for evaluation by the British.

Above: Waffen-SS troops examine a OT-34 flamethrower version of the T-34. Note the 360-degree commander's cupola and separate hatch for the loader which appeared only on the final T-34/76s.

fighting in the former Yugoslavia in the 1990s. Such longevity in a modern major weapon system is unprecedented.

Quite apart from the T-34's obvious technical attributes, it symbolises the desperate Soviet war effort against the Nazi invaders. It was the T-34 that finally blunted the Blitzkrieg, being instrumental in the victories at Stalingrad and Kursk, and it led the advance on Berlin at the end of World War II in Europe. Professor John Erickson eloquently summed up its importance:

'For the Russians, the T-34 was certainly a war-winning weapon. It was superb on the battlefield ... but it represents so much more. It represents the fact they won a stupendous victory over fascism. The fact that it was there in so many thousands and thousands ... is a tribute to the diligence, to the devotion, to the patriotism, to the self-sacrifice not only of the soldiers, but of the population as a whole. It represents ... a triumph in enormous adversity, the kind of adversity that we have never even imagined.'

THE FIRST TANKS

Although the T-34 had the clearest technological advantage over its German opponents in the summer of 1941, in fact it fared badly, as the Soviet armoured forces were at their most disorganised and poorly led. To understand the reasons for this and the massive achievements that led to the turn around in the fortunes of the T-34 – and Soviet Union's war

effort as a whole – it is necessary to examine the basis of both the Soviet tank industry and Soviet armoured doctrine in the inter-war period in some detail.

Tracked armoured fighting vehicles or (as the British called them) tanks, were first used in combat on 15 September 1916 during the Battle of the Somme. While they achieved some limited local tactical successes, these were somewhat dwarfed by the scale of the sacrifice of the British Army in the four-month battle. Despite a military effort unparalleled in British history and the loss of over 400,000 men, British troops advanced no more than 16km (10 miles) at any one point from their start lines at the beginning of the battle, no enemy positions of strategic importance were captured, and there was certainly no breakthrough.

While the British commander, General Sir Douglas Haig, might argue that the battle had been a strategic success in eroding the fighting capacity of the German Army and relieving pressure on the French, what the Somme had really illustrated, on a terrible scale, was the vulnerability of the human being in modern warfare. Technology, particularly the machine-gun, had reduced mobility on the battlefield during World War I to almost zero. Haig did, however, have the prescience to order the production of a further 1000 tanks.

On 20 November 1917, 381 tanks advanced across open ground on a frontage of 9.65km (six miles) around the village of Cambrai. There had been no preliminary artillery barrage which had heralded the British use of tanks. Therefore, the ground was not a morass of shell holes and churned-up mud and the tanks were able to advance rapidly (a relative term, as the speed of a British Mark IV Tank was about 6.4-8km/h [4-5mph]). The Germans retreated in panic in the wake of the tanks which were supported by aircraft operating in a ground-support role. The British captured 7500 prisoners and broke through to a depth of 6.4km (four miles). It was a stunning success compared to previous advances using conventional means which had been measured in hundreds of yards, and had been achieved without the cost of thousands of lives as infantry losses were minimal. The tank had proved to be a weapon that could break the deadlock imposed by the machine-gun and restore a degree of mobility to warfare.

THE RED ARMY'S EARLY EXPERIENCES OF TANK WARFARE

World War I on the Eastern Front, however, had proved to be of a very different character to that in the West. The Russian Imperial Army had fought a war during 1914–17 where

Below: The T-26, based on a Vickers 6.09-tonne (6-ton) tank design, was the Soviet's mainstay in the 1930s. It served in Spain and Finland and was still in service when the Germans invaded in 1941.

advances had been measured in hundreds of miles, not hundreds of yards. Indeed the Brusilov Offensive had proved that there was still a limited role for cavalry. The dominance of the machine-gun – and also barbed wire – had not proved so total in the East. Solving the problem of their supremacy had not been so imperative, and in any case Tsarist Russia's industry was not up to the challenge of producing tanks had they been needed. The British and French had supplied the Russians with some armoured cars, but the armoured fighting vehicle had made little or no impact on the course of the conflict.

The Russian Revolution and subsequent civil war changed all that. The Western Allies supplied the Whites fighting the Bolshevik revolutionaries with Russia's first tanks. These were a collection of British Mark IVs and Whippets and French Renault FTs and St Chamonds. Eventually some of these fell into the hands of the Bolsheviks and it was from these captured foreign vehicles that the Red Army formed its first armoured units. Both the Communist Party and the Red Army High Command immediately appreciated the effectiveness of tanks, and went to great lengths to provide their young army with this type of equipment. They knew that the only solution to providing sufficient tanks was to begin production of their own.

The urgency caused by the demands of the continuing civil war, coupled with an absolute lack of experience in tank design and production, led to the High Command's

decision to copy an existing model captured in the fighting. Two Renault FT tanks had been seized in March 1919 and they were handed over to a special design team at the Izhorsk Factory in Leningrad, which had been set up to specifically copy the Renault design. The first tank produced in Russia, 'Freedom Fighter Comrade Lenin,' rolled out of Izhorsk on 31 August 1920. Fifteen more, designated M-17, were produced by 1922.

The M-17 had no major impact on the Russian Civil War, and nor were they used in a particularly innovative manner. In common with the standard Western doctrine of the time, the M-17 was used purely to support infantry. However, the post-World War I Red Army remained relatively free of the bonds of contemporary military conventions as perceived in the West, and was receptive to new ideas, or at least willing to adapt modern technology to match their recent experiences. The first generation of Soviet military commanders had developed a unique view of warfare and were unconstrained by the Western experience of trench warfare.

The Civil War had taken place over vast distances and involved limited numbers of troops. The Red Army's leaders had learnt to try and integrate tactical operations into a wider strategic plan, setting their objectives deep in the enemy rear. Such ambitious intentions had two prerequi-

Above: A T-26C command tank in Finland during the Winter War. Radio equipment was still limited to company and occasionally platoon commanders in 1939–40, hence the distinctive aerial.

sites: first, the concentration of superior forces at the vital point and second the ability to subsequently exploit the breakthrough by rapid manoeuvre, flanking enemy concentrations, penetrating deep to the rear and then encircling and destroying him. This required a highly mobile force. In the Civil War to a limited extent this had been made up by armoured trains and armoured cars, but the principal exponent of mobile warfare remained horse cavalry. The élite of the Red Army in the Civil War had been the 1st Cavalry Army of Marshal Budenny. Budenny's unit produced a generation of officers who were absolutely convinced of the value of mobility and manoeuvre.

The new Bolshevik nation, however, had been bankrupted by the Civil War and production of tanks had halted in 1922. No new tank models appeared until 1925. The 5.6-tonne (5.5-ton) T-18 (known to the West as the MS-I) was merely an improved M-17 with a 37mm gun. The MS-II and III which followed added little to the original World War I progenitor, the Renault FT, and were obsolete by Western standards. Even given the very limited innovation of these models copied back in 1919, Soviet industry was not yet capable of producing tanks in any great number. Therefore, the Red Army in the 1920s remained largely a 'foot and hoof army'. Its forces were unable to develop tactical successes to the extent where they became strategic victories. The traditional mobile arm was still the cavalry. While the cavalry had managed to retain an effective and important role in World War I on the Eastern Front and the subsequent Civil War, the Red Army was well aware that the nature of warfare had changed. This had been demonstrated to a certain extent by their own experiences of the Civil War and graphically illustrated by what had happened on the Western Front. There could be no doubt that cavalry could no longer function effectively on the modern battlefield against the crushing weight of firepower available to contemporary armies.

TUKHACHEVSKY, DEEP BATTLE AND RED ARMY REFORM

The problem faced by these cavalry officers was how to restore mobility and manoeuvre to warfare. Their answer was the adoption of large mechanised armoured forces and by the late 1920s they had embraced the tank as their weapon of choice. Nonetheless, as Colonel David Glantz, a distinguished historian of Soviet military theory, has

Below: T-26s on the move. The T-26 proved inadequately armoured and suffered heavy losses in Spain, Finland and in the opening months of the German invasion of the Soviet Union in June 1941.

succinctly noted, 'It is, however, one thing to theorise about change and another to actually effect change in practice.'

The 1920s were an era of austerity and retrenchment for the Red Army; there was little money available for equipment and experimental training. An early attempt to resolve this problem and gain access to Western expertise grew out of the Soviet rapprochement with their fellow pariah nation in the international community, Germany. The Soviet Union was shunned for its Communism, and Germany for its perceived responsibility for World War I. The two countries were isolated and shared a fear of their common neighbour, Poland. They were also eager to circumvent the armament restrictions placed upon them by the victors of World War I. The Germans were particularly keen to rebuild the air and tank arms that were forbidden to them under the 1919 Treaty of Versailles; the vast Russian steppes provided a suitable location for experiment far from the prying eyes of the West.

Therefore in 1921 the first links were established between these two unlikely military collaborators: the Red Army and the German Reichswehr. In 1922, as part of the Rapallo Treaty, a firm agreement on secret military cooperation was signed. The programme was expanded in March 1926. An airfield was established at Lipetsk where German pilots trained and new aircraft designs were tested. A Soviet-German tank school was also founded at Kazan on the Volga; Germany funded and provided technical support there for tank tests.

Above: A T-70 light tank. Due to its long cavalry tradition, the Red Army remained true to the concept of the light tank long after experience had demonstrated its vulnerability on the battlefield.

The Soviet Union and Germany continued to exchange observers for military exercises until Hitler put an end to such collaboration in 1934. Soviet soldiers spent years in Germany absorbing German tactical doctrine and strategic thinking and in 1931 German officers attended courses in Moscow. A number of German officers who participated in these exchanges – Model, Guderian and Manstein – gained considerable fame some 10 years or so later through their exploits as panzer commanders.

It is hardly surprising that exposure to German thinking did much to influence the radical reorganisation of the Red Army and particularly within its mechanised forces. The brilliant Red Army Chief of Staff, Mikhail Tukhachevsky, was a keen advocate of the German-Soviet military cooperation programme and was ready to apply what he had learnt – he also drew heavily on other Western thinking, particularly that of the British armour theorists J.F.C. Fuller and Basil Liddell Hart – when he set out create a modern professional Red Army, albeit an army fired with revolutionary enthusiasm.

In 1926 he ordered a complete review of the armed forces and Soviet military doctrines. The result of Tukhachevsky's study appeared in the 1929 Red Army Field Regulations. Here the Soviet military theorists perfected the tactical concept of Deep Battle (*glubokii boi*). Deep Battle was intended to defeat the defensive systems developed in World War I by penetration of the enemy line followed by rapid advance into the enemy rear. Initially Tukhachevsky intended to use the traditional weapons of the civil war, the infantry, artillery and even cavalry, no doubt influenced by the Red Army's absolute paucity in modern weapons such as aircraft and tanks.

In this, his thinking was not much different from that of other countries. Most armies continued to view the tank as a support weapon for the infantry which, despite the ground-breaking experiments in armoured warfare that had taken place in Britain in the early 1920s, remained the armoured doctrine of the British Army and also that of France and the USA.

The Red Army had relied on such principles throughout the 1920s for the use of its limited number of obsolete tanks.

Above: Finnish troops advance with a captured BT-5. The Finnish Army was chronically short of tanks and pressed into service as many captured Soviet tanks as possible.

Soviet operational and tactical theory, however, evolved quickly, and by 1930 the concept of Deep Battle had been adjusted to involve a Red Army with the whole spectrum of mechanised forces, and which in theory could undertake a sophisticated combined arms battle. Infantry, led by tanks and supported by artillery, would penetrate the enemy defences, while aircraft and further artillery pounded the enemy's rear, supported by independent parachute drops and tank forces. The tanks would be used in three echelons: some would lead the initial infantry penetration; others make a rapid short-range exploitation of the breakthrough; and finally a combined tank-mechanised infantry formation would lead the pursuit and encirclement of the enemy.

In 1936 Tukhachevsky expanded Deep Battle into a larger concept known as Deep Operation (*glubokia operatsiia*). Rather than envisaging the penetration of the enemy in a single tactical deep battle, Tukhachevsky envisaged a large number of penetrations and exploitations to a depth of more than 100km (63 miles). Using modern weapons such as tanks and aircraft, the Red Army would overcome the enemy defences to a maximum depth and exploit the successes so quickly that the enemy would be unable to respond adequately. The enemy would be annihilated on its own territory in mobile war with attack viewed as the only means of combat that could bring a decision. The primacy of the offensive became Red Army dogma.

Tukhachevsky recognised that such an offensive strategy required modern equipment. While the concept of Deep Operation was unusual, it was not unique. There are certainly many similarities between it and the German Blitzkrieg, the principal difference being that breakthroughs would be achieved by a series of blows rather than Blitzkrieg's single aimed thrust. Most armies – even those which proposed the most unimaginative use of tanks – saw mechanised forces as a way to penetrate defences and avoid the stalemate of trench warfare. What was unprecedented in Tukhachevsky's reforms was the degree of official sanction he received from the Soviet Union's dictator Joseph Stalin. This support applied both to the freedom Tukhachevsky received to experiment with armoured forces and restructure the Red Army, and to the gearing of a large proportion of the Soviet Union's industrial capacity to provide the weapons, particularly tanks, that Tukhachevsky needed to put his theories into practice.

The 1929 Regulations gave impetus to the creation of armoured formations and a force structure capable of putting theory into practice. In 1930 the Red Army set up an experimental mechanised brigade which combined armour, motorised infantry, artillery and reconnaissance units. Deep Operations, however, required larger formations and by 1932 the number of these brigades had increased to four which constituted the Red Army's first two mechanised corps. This was three years before the Germans created the first panzer divisions. Not only was the Soviet Union the first country to possess large mechanised units, but she also tested them on manoeuvres.

By the time the whole Deep Operation doctrine and use of armoured formations were codified in the 1936 Field Service Regulations, the Red Army had four mechanised corps (renamed tank corps in 1938) made up of a host of mechanised brigades, regiments and battalions. The armoured forces could function at every level of command providing infantry support and particularly a manoeuvre capability for the Red Army. The 1936 Regulations set out the use of the mechanised corps at the highest levels. At the Front Level (the Soviet equivalent of an Army Group) a Shock Army (*udarnaia armiia*) would conduct the penetration operation providing the tactical breakthrough. Then a Mobile Group (*podvizhnaya gruppa*) would exploit the penetration through the enemy defences to operational depths.

THE SHOCK ARMY

It is worth explaining the Soviet concept of the Shock Army in a little more detail. The Shock Army was heavily equipped and specifically trained to make large-scale attacks that punched through the opposing forces' lines. These armies were considerably larger than a normal army, consisting of four to five rifle – that is infantry – corps, one or two mechanised corps, a larger proportion of artillery brigades, and more independent divisional tank and artillery units. A typical Soviet Army of the 1940–41 period might contain two rifle corps, one cavalry corps and one mechanised corps, which may have been larger or smaller depending on the army's location or role. The 1936 Regulations were also instrumental in incorporating mechanised forces throughout the whole army. The Shock Army, with its tank brigades supporting the infantry assault, and the Mobile Group (always made up of mechanised corps) ready to conduct the deep exploitation operation, has formed the basis of Red Army operational doctrine ever since, with the exception of a brief deviation which accounted for much of the Red Army's disastrous performance in the early years of World War II. The basic concept has not changed in 50 years.

THE DEVELOPMENT OF THE SOVIET TANK INDUSTRY

All these Shock Armies and constituent mechanised corps and brigades required tanks, and it is a notable achievement of Soviet industry that it expanded rapidly enough to produce them in the necessary numbers in a such a short period of time. Tukhachevsky's reform programme meant that the Red Army had to be re-equipped and the ground forces totally mechanised. The 1929 Regulations gave direction to these efforts. In July of that year the Red Army General Staff passed a special directive giving priority to the production of tanks. The programme envisaged a wide range of armoured vehicles for use by the reorganised Soviet Army in a variety of roles: tankettes for reconnaissance; light tanks to act as cavalry; medium tanks for the breakthrough during both mobile and positional warfare; and heavy tanks to punch through particularly heavily fortified areas. At this

Below: A BT-5TU Command tank. The BT series was the most successful of the Soviet inter-war tanks designs, using the Christie suspension system, which gave it excellent cross-country performance.

time the Russians had only the T-18 in production, based on the M-17 that had been produced in the Civil War. The requirement was for a wide range and large number of tanks for experimentation. However, the Soviet Union lacked the expertise in the design and production of tanks.

In 1927, to rectify the shortage of designers and engineers, the Red Army had selected promising young engineers from the Russian automotive industry for special instruction in tank design. The initiative was well-timed. By 1930, when the design and production of tanks was beginning to take priority in Soviet industry, the course had produced a cadre of high-class specialists who formed the basic nucleus of Soviet tank designers over the next decade. Before this expertise came on line, the Soviets found themselves trying to accelerate tank production without having any suitable home-grown designs. Therefore, they were forced to buy experimental foreign designs with the intention of producing more sophisticated versions of the best of them in the Soviet Union.

By Western standards the Soviet Union remained considerably underdeveloped in the mid-1920s. Fearing for his country's survival in a world of hostile capitalist powers, Stalin launched a determined and accelerated programme of industrialisation, economic modernisation and collectivisa-

Above: BT-7s drive through a city. The BT was an excellent tank for its day with reasonable armament and superb mobility; however, like the T-26 it was inadequately armoured, suffering accordingly in combat.

tion of agriculture in 1927. The first Five Year Plan, as it was called, proved disastrous when applied to agriculture, but it was remarkably successful in establishing heavy industry in the Soviet Union in just a few years. The plan initially gave priority to heavy industry and machine engineering, as Stalin's predecessor Lenin had dictated in his theory of economic development. During June 1929, a series of car and tractor plants were established in Moscow, Gorky, Stalingrad, Chelybinsk and Yaroslavl. At about this time oil production began in the Uralkuznets basin. To quote David Glantz again: 'It was a short step from producing tractors to producing tanks and the Soviets made that step very quickly.'

The switch in favour of the production of weapons came in 1931. In February Stalin made a speech to the first All-Union Congress of Managers in which he emphasised how crucial catching up economically was for Soviet security:

'One feature of the old Russia was the continual beatings she suffered for falling behind, for backwardness. She was beaten by the Mogul khans. She was beaten by the Turkish

beys. She was beaten by the Swedish feudal lords. She was beaten by the Polish and Lithuanian gentry. She was beaten by the British and French capitalists. She was beaten by the Japanese barons. All beat her – for her backwardness ... We are 50 or 100 years behind the advanced countries. We must make good this distance in 10 years. Either we do this or they crush us.'

Stalin was clearly convinced of the relationship between military power and economic modernisation and there followed a sharp acceleration in military output and military spending. The portion of national production devoted to defence doubled, and by 1932 one quarter of all capital investment in heavy industry and engineering was in defence-related areas. Stalin also adopted Tukhachevsky's 'Great Tank Programme' which the General Staff had approved in August 1931. Tanks had particular priority at the expense of other types of armaments and by 1932 some 30 factories – some purpose built, others converted from tractor or car production – were mass-producing tanks. The leap in output is staggering. At the beginning of 1928 the Red Army had 92 tanks; by January 1935 there were 10,180. While the major concern was tanks, the increase in other weapons is similarly impressive. Tukhachevsky's plan required 15,000 aircraft. In 1930 there were just over 1000. Five years later there were between 4000 and 5000, considerably more than any other country. The first Five Year Plan established the basis of the Soviet tank industry and the large-scale production of tanks continued throughout the second and third Five Year Plans which took the Soviet Union through to the outbreak of World War II.

TANKETTES AND LIGHT TANKS

The tanks produced during the Five Year Plans were of varying quality. In 1930 the early attempt to build a home-grown medium tank, the T-14, failed due to problems with the suspension, automotive parts and inadequate armour. It was, however, ambitiously armed with a 76mm gun – a huge calibre for a tank of the time – which indicated the Soviet interest in gun power. Some of the foreign copies were at least suitable for adaptation into models capable of large-scale production. British designs proved popular and the Soviets bought the remarkably successful Carden-Loyd tankettes and Vickers 6.1-tonne (6-ton) and 12.2-tonne (12-ton) tanks. From the Carden-Loyd design they produced the T-27 tankette. Admittedly the Russian flirtation with the tankette became a blind alley because the tankette was of extremely limited effectiveness on the battlefield. They could be of some use against infantry in the open, but they could not destroy each other, let alone any larger vehicle. However,

the T-27 was cheap and easy to produce in large numbers and it did give the Red Army some familiarity with armour, allowing it to experiment with mechanised forces on manoeuvres.

Of slightly more utility was the T-26 light tank, based on the Vickers 6.1-tonne (6-ton) design which entered production in 1931. When upgunned with a 45mm weapon, the T-26B saw service in the Spanish Civil War. The experiences in Spain led to the provision of better visual equipment and a more sensible distribution of armour on the T-26C. This version was in widespread service in 1941 but proved no match for the German panzers and neither did the T-28 infantry tank which owed much to Vickers' inter-war designs. Its anachronistic layout of a low-velocity 76mm gun in a central turret and two machine-guns in subsidiary bow turrets was also hopelessly outclassed.

CHRISTIE AND THE M1931

In turning to the ideas of American tank designer Walter Christie, the Soviets finally hit upon a winner. In 1928 Christie offered the US Army his new design, the M1931 tank, which carried itself on a set of four large rubber-tyred road wheels that touched the track at top and bottom. These wheels were slung on pivoting lever arms in the hull sides and sprung by large coil springs mounted between the inner and outer thickness of the vehicle hull. The system allowed enormous deflection which enabled it to stand up to the rigours of rough terrain. The vehicle could run on tracks or on the road wheels themselves and it was powered by an enormous V-12 aero-engine, giving the tank extraordinary performance. On wheels it could reach 113km/h (70mph) which was better than many contemporary cars, and it reached 64km/h (40mph) on its tracks. It was not much of a tank since it was unarmed and had armour no thicker than 12mm (0.5in). However, its cross-country performance was incredible and here the M1931 impressed everyone who saw it. The US Army bought five, the Soviets bought two and the Polish Army ordered two. The US Ordnance Department soon fell out with the cantankerous Christie over the contract and his design was passed over in favour of cheaper alternatives. The Poles also cancelled their order, but the Russians did not.

The excellent cross-country performance of Christie's design appealed to the Soviets. Given the antecedents of the Red Army's mechanised forces, it was hardly surprising that they hankered after a tank that could truly replicate the strategic role of cavalry. By buying the two M1931 chassis from Christie and proceeding to virtually copy the design for their new light/medium tank project, they produced a weapon that filled that role perfectly. The Bystrochodyi (Fast Tank) BT was the key Soviet design of the inter-war period and was probably the best tank produced in the mid-1930s. The entire seven-mark BT series faithfully reproduced the winning Christie suspension system, each model giving a

Left: The BT-7 on wheels. The Christie-designed chassis used on the series allowed the tracks to be removed so it could run on wheels. This gave good performance on roads but was of no use in combat.

T-34/76

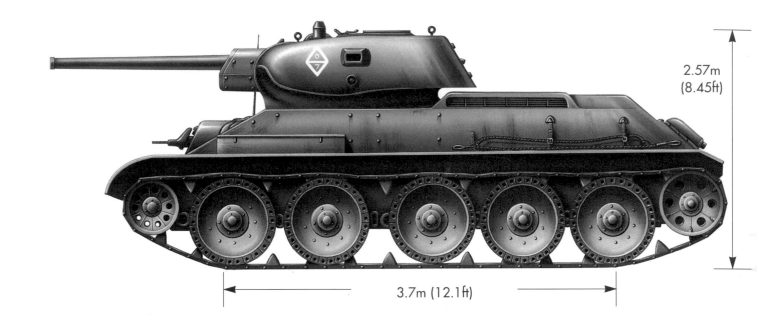

2.57m
(8.45ft)

3.7m (12.1ft)

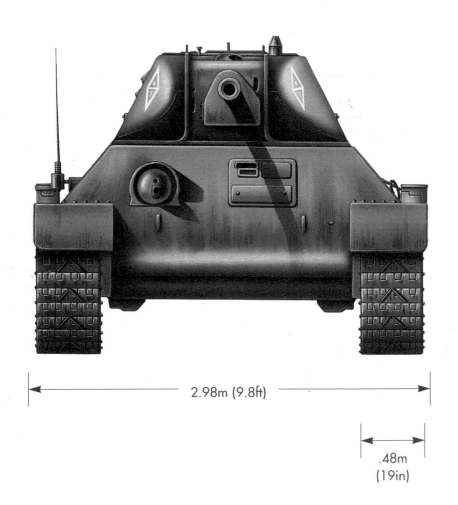

2.98m (9.8ft)

.48m
(19in)

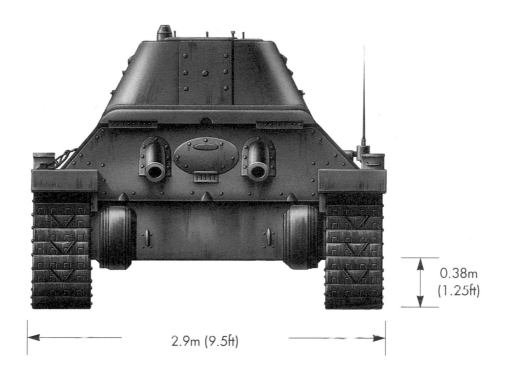

0.38m
(1.25ft)

2.9m (9.5ft)

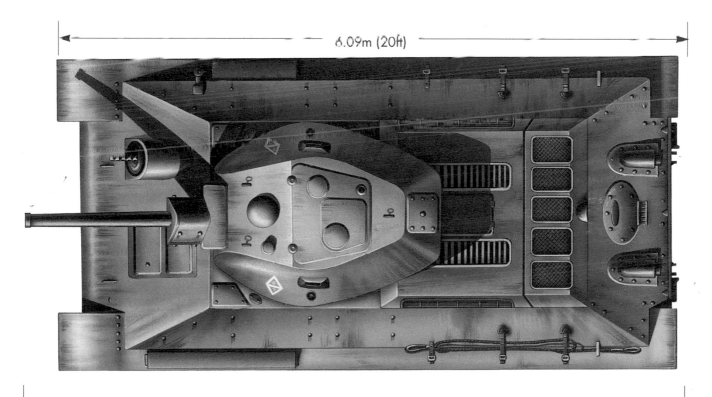

6.09m (20ft)

6.58m (21.6ft)

cross-country performance that astonished all foreign observers with its resilience and robustness. The Russian tank retained Christie's dual track/road wheel capability and this arrangement consumed vital space that could have been used inside the vehicle. However, regarding cross-country performance and speed, the suspension did all that was asked of it.

The BT was steadily upgunned. The initial model received a 37mm main armament. The BT-5 was given a 45mm high-velocity gun in 1932 and some versions of the BT-7 received a 76mm weapon in 1938. Although it was adequately armed, it performed disappointingly in Spain, Manchuria and Finland, largely due to its poor protection and cramped main turret. However, it should be remembered that BT was a seminal design and the most advanced tank of its time.

The story of the engine development of the BT tank is closely linked to the subsequent work on the T-34. In 1934 the design bureau of the Kirov factory in Leningrad was working on the T-29-S tank which did not get past the experimental stage. However, the project had involved a young engineer Mikhail Koshkin who during 1936 was transferred to the Komintern Factory in Kharkov to take up the position of chief designer. Given Koshkin's age, this appointment was remarkable, but he soon proved his worth. The Kharkov design team were working on improvements for the BT. Under Koshkin they produced the BD-2 diesel engine for the BT-5. This new engine reduced the BT's fuel consumption and increased the tank's range while maintaining its performance. The efficient and strain-resistant BD-2 engine was encased in aluminium which was another pioneering development. The engine was the predecessor of the V-2 diesel of the T-34, and Koshkin would head the T-34 design team. Soviet mechanisation was not perfect: the tanks were still lightly armed and relied on speed for protection and radio communication – where provided – was notoriously unreliable. The initial mechanised corps structure had proved too unwieldy and Tukhachevsky had to reduce the corps' size in 1935. Another problem was that the average Soviet soldier was ill-educated and lacked experience in maintenance. Consequently equipment soon broke down and wore out at a rapid rate. Nonetheless, by the mid-1930s the Soviet Union led the world in the production, planning and fielding of mechanised forces. They had not only set up the first large scale mechanised units but also tested them on manoeuvres. The Soviets also possessed in the BT tank, a vehicle to which there was no competitor of comparable quality.

In comparison with the Germany Army – the Soviet Union's most likely opponents – the Red Army was well ahead in both theoretical and practical experience in mechanised warfare. Guderian and the panzer theorists in Germany had received virtually no support compared with the whole-hearted support that Tukhachevsky had received from Stalin and the Soviet Government. Tank production in Germany had taken a back seat to the Luftwaffe, and the Soviet Union had a considerable advantage over Germany in the mid-1930s. That advantage, however, was soon swept away.

THE PURGE

From 1934 onwards Stalin had systematically eliminated potential rivals throughout the Soviet Government. By 1937 only the Red Army remained untouched. Historians have

Below: A T-34 Model 1940. This version entered full-scale production in the autumn of 1940. Unusually, these early T-34s enjoyed a high level of craftsmanship in their manufacture.

Above: Two T-34 Model 1941s carrying prominent bundles of fascines used for crossing trenches. Note the towing cable attached to the front of the lead tank.

struggled to explain why Stalin turned on the Soviet military with such ferocity. David Glantz suggests that while the Soviet dictator loved the Red Army, he distrusted professional soldiers. Stalin valued loyalty, orthodoxy, and intellectual subservience, and independent thought disturbed him. Certainly Tukhachevsky had an independence of thought; he was also outspoken and disliked the military amateurs of the Party. Stalin's only close military associate was Defence

Commissar Marshal Kliment Voroshilov. Voroshilov, an 'unimaginative crony' and (according to Nikita Khrushchev) 'the biggest bag of shit in the army', appears to have encouraged Stalin's prejudices as he 'resented Tukhachevsky's intellectual brilliance because it highlighted his own limited abilities as a commander'.

Whatever the case, Tukhachevsky was arrested on 27 May 1937, but was certainly innocent of the charge of planning to overthrow the state at the head of an invading German Army. A confession was brutally beaten out of him and seven other senior Red Army officers were arrested at the same time. They were tried and found guilty on 11 June and shot that day. There was no elaborate show trial; Voroshilov merely announced Tukhachevsky's execution the following day.

The net soon spread and over the next four years right up to the German invasion Soviet officers disappeared with alarming regularity. Of an estimated 75–80,000 officers, 30,000 were imprisoned or executed. This included three out of five marshals; all 11 deputy defence commissars; all the commanders of the Soviet Union's Military Districts; 14 out of 16 Army Commanders; 60 out of 67 Corps Commanders and down through the lower ranks. Out of 85 senior officers on the Military Council, 71 were dead by 1941. Only nine escaped the purges entirely. A whole generation of commanders, military administrators and factory managers had been wiped out. As General Konstantin Rokossovsky – who later commanded the Don Front at the Battle of Stalingrad – said during his two years spent in prison from 1938–40 on evidence apparently provided by a man who had died 20 years before: 'This is worse than when artillery fires on its own troops.' Young men were thrust into positions of responsibility for which they were not ready. Training and maintenance suffered. Deep Battle and Deep Operations and Tukhachevsky's mechanised force structure suddenly fell into disrepute and many of Tukhachevsky's writings were recalled and burnt.

There seems little method in the selection of those removed, although Tukhachevsky's circle was systematically eliminated. The fact that senior officers did not owe their career to Stalin seems to be the only constant criterion for their extermination. One of the few formations with which Stalin had close links was the 1st Cavalry Division which he had helped direct during the Civil War. Of those nine survivors of the purge of the Military Council, seven had served with the 1st Cavalry Division, including Voroshilov, the able Marshal Semyon Timoshenko and, thankfully for the

Below: The T-34 Model 1940 in August 1941 with a cast turret designed by V. Buslov and V. Nitsenko. Easier to manufacture than the welded type, tanks with cast turrets were produced at Gorki.

Above: A T-34 Model 1941 with the commander navigating, head out of the turret. The clumsy one-piece hatch restricted the commander's view; fighting with the hatch open was virtually impossible.

salvation of the Soviet Union, Georgi Zhukov, possibly the best but certainly the most successful commander of World War II. Marshal Semyon Budenny, the most famous cavalry-man of them all, had a close escape. He forcefully resisted arrest and managed to phone Stalin directly, so being saved from the fate that met most of his colleagues.

The purges certainly had an adverse effect on combat performance of the Red Army after 1937–38, for, quite apart from the decapitation of the leadership, the balance of power shifted in the military. After a decade of attempts led by Tukhachevsky to win back independent control and to professionalise the Red Army, the purges brought back close political supervision. In August 1937 Stalin ordered the 'Bolshevisation' of the army and appointed Lev Mekhlis, the editor of *Pravda*, head of the Red Army's Main Political Directorate. In the same month that Tukhachevsky was arrested, Voroshilov reintroduced political deputies or commissars into all units above divisional strength. Mekhlis kept up the terror's momentum by insisting that the commissars in every unit play a substantial military role. It is estimated that some 73 per cent of political officers had no military training, yet they had soon spread down even to platoon level. This restricted the independence of commanders, demoralising officers and making them excessively cautious as any slip might lead to arrest for infringing the party line. This political control led to most officers sticking strictly to the rule book. Talk of Deep Battle or of Tukhachevsky's theories was deemed counter-revolutionary and military professionalism came to be considered as 'bourgeois expertise'. To quote historian Richard Overy: 'The result was the triumph of military illiteracy over military science, of political conformity over military initiative.'

The Party also imposed its own ideological view of warfare, considering that wars were decided not by technology and modern weapons, but by the masses and their motivation. Tukhachevsky's emphasis – much influenced by Fuller and Liddell Hart – on the importance of a single weapon system, the tank, was dismissed as a symptom of the class-bound nature of bourgeois armies. The Communist Party believed that the chief instrument of war remained the infantry and therefore, it was comparatively simple to turn the tank into a pure infantry support weapon. This was well-illustrated by the *Pravda* editorial of February 1939 to mark the twentieth anniversary of the foundation of the Frunze Military Academy:

'Military thought in the capitalist world has got into a bind. The dashing "theories" about a lightning war, or about

Above: This shot of a T-34, either a Model 1940 or Model 1941, illustrates the overhang at the turret's rear, which deflected incoming rounds on to the turret ring.

small, select armies of technicians, or about the air war which can replace all other military operations; all these theories arise from the bourgeoisie's deathly fear of proletarian revolution. In its mechanical way, the imperialist bourgeoisie overrates equipment and underrates man.'

This thinking goes some way to explain the disastrous performance of Soviet armour and misplaced faith in the efficacy of mass wave attacks by infantry which proved so costly and ineffectual in the initial fighting after the German invasion of 1941.

PRACTICAL EXPERIENCE

The difficulties and disillusionment with tanks and large-scale mechanised forces went beyond the politicisation of the army and the destruction of a substantial proportion of its leadership in the purges. Real experience also caused Soviet commanders to question the utility of large-scale mechanised forces and rethink the role of the tank. The Soviet experience in the Spanish Civil War, which occurred concurrently with the first wave of Stalin's purge of the military, did as much to discredit massed tank operations as did Marshal Tukhachevsky (and his ideas) becoming persona non grata. The erroneous conclusions that the Soviet officers

in Spain drew from the conflict further slowed the development of the Soviet armoured forces. However, the conflict did lead to technical advances that were central to the success of the T-34 which was built as a direct result of the experiences of Spain.

In 1937 the Soviet Union sent a fairly large armoured contingent to Spain of 50 or so tanks supporting the Republicans. The Soviet tanks suffered all sorts of problems during the fighting. The BTs were an effective combination of speed and gun power but they tended to be regarded as universal tanks capable of both the cavalry role for which they were designed and also infantry support. The BT and T-26, which also saw extensive service in Spain, were both lightly armoured. The support of infantry required the tank to move at the pace of a foot soldier which made it extremely vulnerable in the face of anti-tank guns. Consequently the BTs and T-26s suffered heavily. Methods of using tanks which deprived them – particularly in the case of the BT – of their main advantage of mobility and exposed them to enemy anti-tank gunners made little sense.

Conversely, when attacking fortified positions in depth, the tanks tended to outrun their supporting troops, and the defending infantry could destroy the tanks with relative ease. This was not the cavalry role for which the BT was built. The situation was little helped by the fact that the Soviet crews were often improvised and could not communicate with the Spanish infantry they were supposed to be supporting.

THE ABOLITION OF THE TANK CORPS

The Chief of Armoured Forces, General Dmitri Pavlov, returned home with an extremely pessimistic attitude towards the viability of massed armour and the general usefulness of tanks. He concluded that Tukhachevsky's new mechanised formations were too large and clumsy to control, far too vulnerable to artillery fire and had great difficulties in penetrating enemy defences, thus making the conduct of Deep Operations impossible. In July 1939 a special commission was convened to examine Pavlov's criticism of the Red Army armoured doctrine and force structure. It was chaired by another of Stalin's cronies, Assistant Defence Commissar Kulik, and included few experienced tank men. It concluded that the tank corps should be reduced to an infantry support role and so the Tank Corps was formally abolished in 1940. The seven mechanised corps were ordered to disband (although two survived in practice) and their vehicles were distributed among the infantry corps. In their place, the largest armoured formation became the new, apparently 'more balanced' motor rifle division, with a mere 37 tanks. This was hastily complemented by a new motorised division in 1940 containing 275 tanks. The Soviet concepts of mechanised warfare and force structure had regressed to a more primitive, less ambitious level than in 1936.

Below: One of the many T-34s captured by the Germans in 1941. The engine access plate and exhaust pipes on either side can be clearly seen at the rear of the tank.

The Soviet Union was also involved in bitter fighting elsewhere at the tail-end of the 1930s. In May 1939, at Khalkin Gol on the border of the Mongolian People's Republic with China, the Japanese provoked a series of skirmishes with the Red Army which soon escalated. In mid-June, Lieutenant-General Georgi Zhukov was sent to command the rapidly growing Soviet forces in the region facing some 75,000 Japanese troops and 200 tanks. By the time he was ready to attack, Zhukov had been reinforced to the level of 100,000 men and 700 tanks. Among his tanks were some brand new BT-7M tanks with 76mm high-velocity guns and good engines. This version of the BT is often regarded as the test bed for the T-34. Zhukov fought a battle of encirclement, decisively defeating the Japanese and at the same time demonstrating the viability of Tukhachevsky's theory and force structure. It was the one bright spot for the Soviet military in this period; no one in Moscow seems to have taken much notice.

RECREATING THE ARMOURED FORCE

As Europe plunged into war in September 1939, the Soviets soon lost confidence in their decision to abolish their tank corps. Admittedly the one mechanised corps used in the Soviet invasion of Finland in November 1939 performed extremely badly and ended up providing merely infantry support. During the 106-day Winter War, Soviet tanks fared little better in this role than they had in Spain, even considering the paucity of Finnish anti-tank weaponry, largely consisting of Molotov cocktails. The Soviets lost some 1600 tanks in the brief but brutal fighting.

The Soviet Union also lost much military credibility due to the failures and difficulties in Finland. This had a cumulative effect as foreign observers were already inclined to dismiss the Red Army due to the ravages of the purges. Much of the derisive attitude taken by Hitler and some of his generals towards Soviet military competence resulted from the purges and the Red Army's poor showing in Finland.

Conversely the performance of the German Army in Poland provoked a considerable degree of awe in the Soviet Command. This was compounded by the stunning success of the Wehrmacht in France in May 1940. As one Soviet general commented: 'My God, they picked up on our ideas and are effectively implementing them while we have gone in the opposite direction.' The Soviet Command then tried to hastily recreate the armoured force structure that had been so brutally torn apart since 1937. When the Germans invaded in June 1941 the reforms were incomplete. Tanks were still deployed in 'penny packets' and the Soviet commanders were unable to mass enough to resist the panzer spearheads successfully. Perhaps the only positive element was that by June 1941 the Red Army had one tank that could blunt the Blitzkrieg. This was the T-34 which would have to be properly used in combat to prove truly effective.

CHAPTER 2

Design and Layout of the T-34

The design and layout of the T-34 combined firepower, armour protection and manoeuvrability almost perfectly. One drawback, however, was the lack of space in the T-34/76 (a feature of most Soviet tanks), which hampered the efficiency of the crew.

General Dmitri Pavlov drew mixed conclusions from the operational performance of Soviet tanks in the Spanish Civil War. His belief that the employment of massed armour was ineffective had a baleful effect on the Red Army's mechanised forces and serious consequences in 1941. Although it is not known for certain who was responsible for the Soviet High Command's decision to commission a new tank design, Pavlov is easily the most likely candidate. He was head of the Directorate of Armoured Forces (ABTU) and therefore heavily involved with the whole re-evaluation of the uses and design requirements of future Soviet tanks that stemmed from lessons learnt during the war in Spain. Both of these factors point towards Pavlov as the originator of the observations which concluded that the Red Army needed a new tank. If this is the case, the disastrous reforms he initiated were at least partially offset by his astute proposals that culminated in the building of the T-34, although he was never a passionate advocate of the design.

The Spanish Civil War provoked some very important developments in Soviet tank design. The Soviet BT and T-26 tanks' vulnerability made it clear that anti-tank weapons had improved considerably in both their quality and effectiveness. The current generation of tanks no longer maintained their dominance over opposing arms; they had lost their ability to withstand fire directed against them. The tanks' armoured protection was quite simply inadequate and therefore the Soviets set to work producing a so-called 'shell-proof' tank with a far higher degree of survivability.

Left: A T-34/85. This Czech-built model was captured during the Korean War and subsequently shipped off to the United Kingdom. It is now housed at the Bovington Tank Museum.

Above: This is a view of the front hull of a T-34/85 captured in the Korean War. It gives a good view of the ball-mounted hull machine-gun position and the driver's hatch in the front glacis plate.

What the Soviets meant by 'shell-proof' was an armoured vehicle that could not just take hits from small arms fire and shell splinters but also from small-calibre artillery and contemporary anti-tank weapons. More specifically, they wanted a tank capable of resisting a round from a 37mm gun at any range and a 76mm weapon at ranges in excess of 1000m (1100yds). Also Soviet tanks had shown an alarming propensity to burst into flames when hit, largely due to their petrol engines, and this stimulated a Soviet interest in diesel engines, the fuel for which was considerably less explosive.

As the BT had proved so vulnerable in Spain, Pavlov wanted a replacement tank, essentially an improved version of the BT-IS. He gave the task to a design team at the Kharkov

Locomotive Factory (also known as the Komintern Factory) in November 1937. His requirements were for a fast vehicle which used the convertible wheel/track system and Christie suspension of the BT family. The new 20.2-tonne (20-ton) tank, designated the A-20, was to have a 45mm gun and 20mm (0.8in) armour. It was not a particularly revolutionary design specification but Pavlov evidently wanted to combine heavier protection with the existing fire power and mobility of the BT series. The Kharkov factory, however, eventually delivered to the Director of Armoured Forces something very special in return.

KOSHKIN AND THE KHARKOV DESIGN TEAM

The head of the Kharkov design bureau, Mikhail Koshkin, had been transferred to the factory to work on improvements on the BT in 1936. Koshkin had assembled a talented and experienced design team. His deputy, Alexsandr Morozov, was responsible for the power train and Morozov had worked for some time with Koshkin. He was closely connected with the development of the new V-2 diesel engine which had been first used on the BT-8 and the Voroshilovets artillery tractor. The suspension team was led by Nikolai Kucherenko and P. Vasihev who had been part of the T-29-4 test tank project, which had examined the applicability of the Christie-type suspension on medium tanks that were considerably heavier than the BT. M. Tarshinov was responsible for the armour layout of the new tank and had been involved in the work on the BT-IS and the BT-SV test tanks at Kharkov under Koshkin's predecessor, A. Firsov. The

Below: The Christie supension system on a T-34/85. Each wheel was hung on one of these independently mounted sprockets which transversely swung on a vertical coil spring located in the hull.

BT-SV project had made ground-breaking use of 25mm (1in) of sloping armour. Firsov had disappeared in the wave of purges that had devastated the BT designers. While Firsov was a talented designer and his arrest and that of much of his team was a criminal waste of talent, Koshkin's resulting promotion was one of the few examples of the purges achieving something positive, albeit by chance.

They presented a wooden model of the A-20 to the Defence Council of the Soviet of People's Commissars (Sovet Narodnykh Komissarov, or SNK) in May 1938. However, Koshkin and his design team had a number of doubts about the A-20 design specification; in particular they were unenthusiastic about the need for the convertible wheel/track feature. Koshkin argued that it added needless weight to the design, and combat experience had shown the feature to be pointless. As he and Morozov explained in a letter to the Soviet High Command:

'In view of the tactical reluctance to employ BT tanks in the wheeled mode, added to the difficulties in the technology associated with producing a tank which is able to travel on both wheel and tracks as required, it is suggested that future efforts should be directed towards the development of a less complex vehicle, running on tracks alone and

P 11449

employing the coil spring (Christie) suspension of the BT series.'

Koshkin also judged that the tank's armour needed to be at least 30mm (1.2in) thick to withstand existing and future threats. He considered that the 45mm gun was also inadequate and that a considerably larger 76mm weapon was needed to penetrate enemy tanks that were equally well-protected. He made these points strongly at a presentation at which Joseph Stalin was present. Stalin was evidently impressed by some of Koshkin's arguments and the Main Military Council subsequently gave permission for the Kharkov factory to build a prototype both of the A-20, and also of an heavier up-armoured and up-gunned version designated the A-30.

The wheel/track issue remained unresolved. The unnecessary combination of tracks and road wheels was unduly heavy and the complex technology involved increasingly convinced the Kharkov design team that the system would hamper mass-production and cause difficulties with maintenance. Simplicity was always a virtue when considering the educational standard of the average Red Army soldier. Therefore, on their own initiative, Koshkin and Morozov designed a heavier purely tracked medium tank based around the A-30 which incorporated the suggestions that

Above: A T-34 Model 1940 at a German proving ground during World War II. Note the large turret hatch, L-11 gun, and apparent hits on the turret side of the tank.

Koshkin had made to the Main Military Council. They submitted drawings of a 19.2-tonne (19-ton) tank, the A-32 (also called the T-32) to a conference on medium tank design in August 1938. The Defence Committee and Stalin approved the project and demanded the production and evaluation of a prototype of the A-32 as soon as possible.

The process that led to the approval of the A-32 illustrated the fickle but occasionally inspired influence of Joseph Stalin on the Soviet Union's military matters. The Main Military Council had criticised the A-32 because it did not follow the original ABTU requirement for the wheel/track feature. Such was the shadow cast over senior Soviet military circles by Stalin's purges and the evident dangers of independent thought, that none of the council were willing to risk defending the project for fear that they might provoke the terrible wrath of the state. Stalin, however, had listened to those tank men who had fought in Spain and who considered that the BTs and the whole current generation of Soviet tanks were too lightly armoured. Stalin took their concerns on board and seeing the logic of Koshkin's argument that the weight saved by losing the wheel/track feature could be used to add extra protection, he backed the A-32. This meant that the Kharkov design team had three projects on their hands, the A-20, A-30 and A-32.

THE PROTOTYPES

The prototype of the A-20 was further advanced and stuck closely to ABTU specification. The 18.2-tonne (18-ton) design retained the wheel/track configuration of the BT series. Like its BT forebears, it ran on four pairs of road wheels powered by the new compact and powerful 500bhp V-2 diesel tank engine. The chassis was based on that of the BT-7M. The A-20 was armed with the 45mm high-velocity gun that had armed most of the BT series, as well a co-axial and hull-mounted machine-guns. The shape of the tank, however, was more interesting as it provided the first glimpse of the hull and turret shape that was adopted in the T-34. The A-20 had a new 25mm- (1in-) thick rolled armour plate turret. The A-20's wide T-shaped glacis plate was set at 60 degrees. The hull overhung the tracks and the hull sides above track level were angled and 25mm (1in) thick. This conformed to the same specifications of another attempt to produce a 'shell proof' tank, the T-46-5 (or Izdeliye 111). This 32.3-tonne (32-ton) tank had reached the prototype stage and subsequently been cancelled. However, its armour protection schemes had some influence on the A-20.

The attempt to up-gun the A-20 in the shape of the A-30 soon proved to be a dead end. The design team tried to place the short-barrelled 76.2mm (L/30.5) gun used on the BT-7 in the A-20 turret. This failed comprehensively because the turret was far too small for the larger weapon, making it extremely difficult to operate. More fundamentally, the turret ring could not absorb the recoil of the 76.2mm gun. The basic impracticability of the project ensured that the A-30 was quietly dropped.

The A-32 was a far more promising design and was a major development on the BT. The complex wheel/track system was finally dropped, although the tank retained the Christie suspension system and, as it did not have to move on wheels, a considerable weight saving was made and therefore the amount of armour on the new hull shape could be increased to between 30 and 60mm (1.2in and 2.4in) without violating the weight limit imposed by the tactical and technological criteria for the project. The designers also gave the A-32 a new steering system which used the conventional method of levers rather than a steering wheel as had been used in the BTs and the A-20. The Soviets had discovered on the BT series that while a steering wheel was certainly not the best method of steering a tracked vehicle, it had proved impossible to steer a wheeled vehicle with levers. The road wheels were increased to five. Finally, true to Koshkin's original proposal for an tank with a larger gun as well as thicker armour, it was given a 76.2mm main gun. Prototypes for both the A-20 and A-32 were ready by July 1939 and were sent to the Scientific Test Institute of Tank Technology (NIIBT) at

Kubinka where they both proved mechanically reliable and superior to all other models. The A-20's performance without tracks was poor but, like the A-32, with tracks it was very satisfactory. Meanwhile on 1 September 1939 – the day Germany invaded Poland – both the A-20 and A-32 appeared in a special display of new Red Army tanks held for the Main Military Council along with the Red Army's newest tanks: the KV heavy tank; the expensive and complex T-50 light tank; and T-40 amphibious tank. The inclusion of the two tanks in the display indicated official satisfaction with the design though there was no consensus amongst the Main Military Council in respect of the A-20 and A-32. Koshkin was quite vehement in his belief that the A-32 was the superior model. He reckoned that the A-32 ought to be considered a universal tank which should replace a whole raft of Soviet tank types and fulfil the roles of the BT, T-26 and T-28 medium tank. Its disadvantage was that it was comparatively expensive and some of the council expressed concern that the A-32 cost three times as much as the T-26 light tank. Pavlov supported the A-20, the product of his initial ABTU design specification.

THE UP-ARMOURED A-32

The issue was finally settled at a meeting of the Defence Committee of the SNK on 19 December 1939. The debate turned to the latest reports from the initial fighting in Finland against the Soviet Union invasion on 30 November. The experience appeared somewhat similar to that in Spain and Khalkin Gol. The reports stressed the vulnerability of Soviet tanks to Finnish anti-tank guns. Given that the Finns possessed virtually no anti-tank weapons, this was really a testament to the extreme bravery of the Finnish infantry's tank-killing squads and the sound use of their very limited artillery. However, there was no doubt that the generation of Soviet tanks seeing service in Finland were proving to be inadequately protected. In addition, their weaponry – usually the standard 45mm tank gun or the short low-velocity 76mm – had proved inadequate against Finnish bunkers. There was no tank-to-tank combat for the report to draw upon as the handful of obsolete Vickers tanks that Finland possessed were only used once in brief counter-attack in February 1940.

Koshkin told the committee that, after considering these developments, his team had prepared estimates that the A-32 could be up-armoured even further without an unacceptable loss of performance and mobility. He produced drawings and models to back up his case, and convinced Stalin, who was in the chair. As a result, the committee approved the up-armoured version of the A-32 medium tank as a replacement for the BT and T-28. It is a measure of the serious situation in Europe at the end of 1939 that the committee ordered into production a project that Koshkin had made quite clear was incomplete: a prototype had not yet been built. Representatives of the Committee for Medium Industry were

T-34 TANK MODEL 1942

1. Armoured gun mantlet
2. F-34 76.2mm main gun
3. Co-axial Degtaryev DT 7.62mm machine gun
4. DT 7.62mm machine gun ammunition
5. Turret hatch
6. Port for signal flages and flare gun
7. Turret hatch lock
8. Rear turret access for main gun removal
9. Gunners PT-5 periscope
10. Periscope sight
11. Range scale elevation knob
12. Telescopic sight

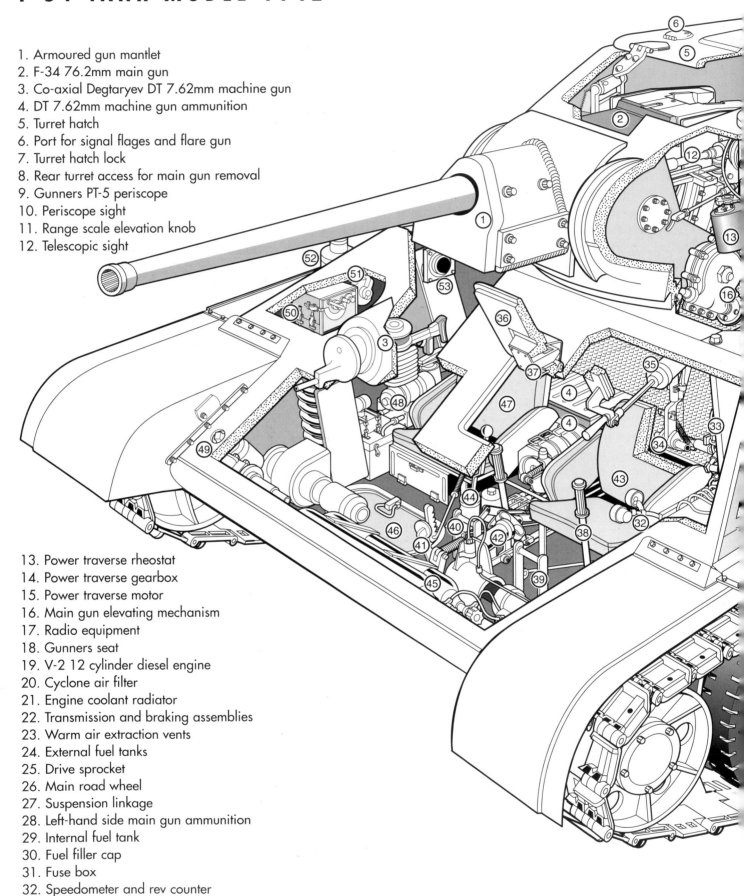

13. Power traverse rheostat
14. Power traverse gearbox
15. Power traverse motor
16. Main gun elevating mechanism
17. Radio equipment
18. Gunners seat
19. V-2 12 cylinder diesel engine
20. Cyclone air filter
21. Engine coolant radiator
22. Transmission and braking assemblies
23. Warm air extraction vents
24. External fuel tanks
25. Drive sprocket
26. Main road wheel
27. Suspension linkage
28. Left-hand side main gun ammunition
29. Internal fuel tank
30. Fuel filler cap
31. Fuse box
32. Speedometer and rev counter
33. Fuel bleeder cock

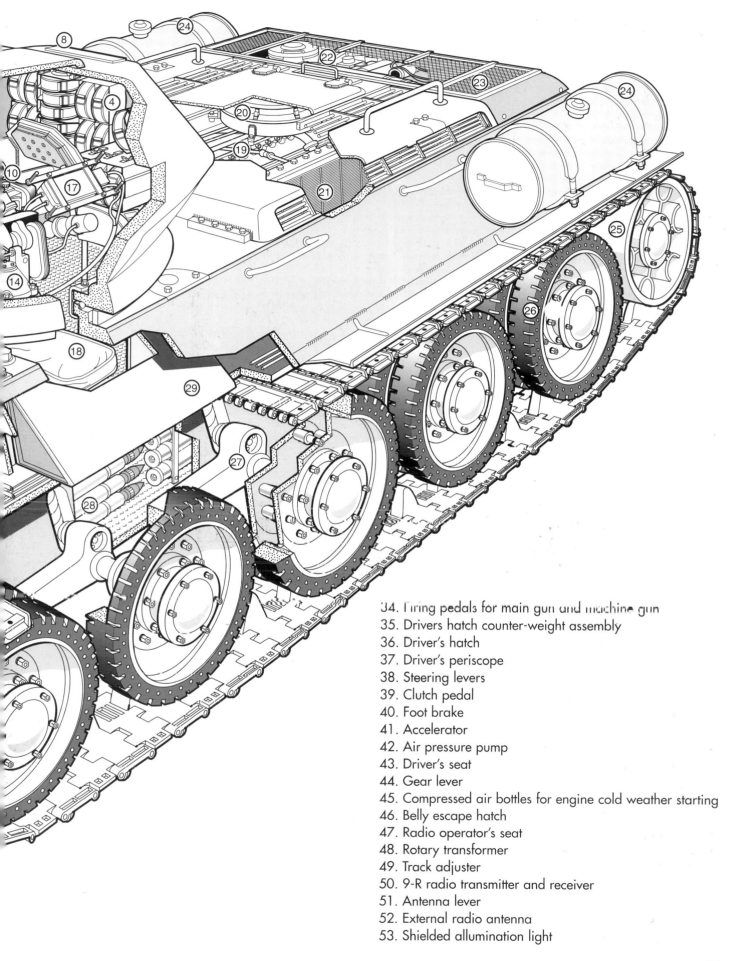

34. Firing pedals for main gun and machine gun
35. Drivers hatch counter-weight assembly
36. Driver's hatch
37. Driver's periscope
38. Steering levers
39. Clutch pedal
40. Foot brake
41. Accelerator
42. Air pressure pump
43. Driver's seat
44. Gear lever
45. Compressed air bottles for engine cold weather starting
46. Belly escape hatch
47. Radio operator's seat
48. Rotary transformer
49. Track adjuster
50. 9-R radio transmitter and receiver
51. Antenna lever
52. External radio antenna
53. Shielded allumination light

THE ENGINE

The engine was mounted at the rear of the hull and was flanked by cooling radiators. There was a cooling fan in the centre. It was the V-type four stroke 12-cylinder, water-cooled diesel that had been developed for the BT-7M. The 3.8 litre (0.84 gallon) version fitted to the T-34 could produce an impressive 493bhp at 1800rpm and gave an excellent power-to-weight ratio of 18.8bhp per tonne (17.9bhp per ton). This gave the T-34 a road speed of 54km/h (34mph) and a cross-country speed of between 16 and 25km/h (10 and 15.62mph) depending on terrain at an average 1.84 litres per kilometre (0.65 gallons per mile). This improved considerably on the road. The V-2 also gave an increased range of operation of 464km (290 miles) compared to tanks powered by conventional petrol internal combustion engines. The use of diesel also reduced the fire risk. The main fuel tank was in the hull. Auxiliary tanks could be carried in four cylinder tanks on the side of the hull and two smaller ones on the rear hull plate.

The transmission was positioned at the rear. Therefore, the driving/fighting compartment was not cluttered by a drive train running to the front of the tank, as was the case of most Western tanks. The Soviets never developed a system comparable to the excellent Maybach transmission used on German tanks and the transmission proved troublesome throughout much of the war. This was particularly a problem in the earlier units, so much so that some tanks went into battle with spare transmissions secured to the engine compartment deck by steel cables.

told that the High Command wanted 200 built in the following year. All that remained was that the new tank be given a name.

THE FIRST T-34S

The heavy tank design bureau in Leningrad had reversed many years of Soviet practice by naming their new tank the Kliment Voroshilov or KV after the egregious Defence

Above: Rear of a T-34/76 showing the engine decks and transmission cover. Screwed-on cover plates allowed easy access for repairs, which was important given the unreliable nature of the T-34's transmission.

Commissar. With some courage Koshkin told Voroshilov that the new tank should not be named after another hero of the Soviet Union; rather they should return to using the traditional designations. Koshkin suggested the designation 'T-34' to commemorate the 1934 state decree ordering a massive expansion of the Soviet armoured forces. It was also the year that Koshkin had had his first ideas about the new tank. Koshkin's proposal was accepted.

Once the team received official sanction to build a purely tracked medium tank they had returned much of their design for the A-32 to the drawing board, realising that not only did the T-34 require thicker armour than the A-32, but it also needed more firepower and a reliable transmission, especially since transmission problems were the bane of most World War II tanks. Morozov, head of the transmission group, devoted considerable time and effort to the problem.

Below: A captured T-34/85 from the Korean War. Particularly prominent on this photograph are the external long-range fuel tanks at either side of the exhausts.

The two prototypes were ready by January 1940, and Koshkin took the two tanks on a gruelling trial march which more than proved the hardiness of the design. They travelled from Kharkov to Moscow where the tank was presented to the Red Army. The tanks were then sent to Finland for combat tests against the Finnish positions on the Mannerheim Line, but by the time they arrived the Winter War had ended. Therefore they had to content themselves with demonstrating the power of the T-34's armament by demolishing some captured Finnish bunkers. There were further firing trials in Minsk and then it was onto Kiev and finally back to Kharkov. This was a round trip of 2880km (1800 miles), and February and March were chosen due to the particularly harsh weather at that time of year.

During June the drawings were completed and mass-production began. The first production tank of the T-34

Model 1940 finally rolled out of Kharkov in September 1940. The Kharkov design team and factory had produced a tank superior to all its contemporaries and it struck an almost perfect balance between armour, mobility and firepower. Most importantly, the T-34 gave the Soviet Union a considerable technological lead over Germany.

The Soviets were well-aware of their technological lead, having been given access to German tank technology by the bizarre nature of European diplomacy in 1939–40. As part of the Nazi-Soviet Pact of 23 August 1939, Hitler sent the Red Army several PzKpfw III tanks, which, according to Wehrmacht officers, were the best German tanks available. The Soviets reckoned that the PzKpfw III was over-engineered and over-comfortable, while considerably inferior to the T-34 on the all-important areas of armament, mobility and protection.

The brilliant German panzer commander General Heinz Guderian provides an interesting German perspective of this arrangement. The Germans were confident that their qualitative superiority in tanks would make up for the Red Army advantage in tank numbers when they invaded the Soviet Union. However, as Guderian recalled:

'... one curious incident made me at least slightly dubious concerning the relative superiority of our armoured equipment. In the spring of 1941 Hitler had specifically ordered that a Russian military commission be shown over our tank schools and factories; in this order he had insisted that nothing be concealed from them. The Russian officers in question firmly refused to believe the Panzer IV [Germany's latest and largest tank] was in fact our heaviest tank. They said repeatedly that we must be hiding our newest models from them, and complained that we were not carrying out Hitler's order to show them everything. The military commission was so insistent on this point that eventually our manufacturers and Ordnance Office officials concluded: "It seems that the Russians must already possess better and heavier tanks than we do".'

As Guderian laconically concluded, the 'riddle of the new Russian model was solved' when the German armour ran into the T-34 on the battlefield in July 1941. The T-34 design team had little cause for celebration, however, as Mikhail Koshkin's health deteriorated due to the pneumonia he had caught during the gruelling winter test drive. He died on 26 September 1940 and the Soviet Union lost probably the

Below: The driver's position. Note the manual clutch pedal and foot brake, the two steering levels on either side of the seat, and two compressed-air bottles used to start the diesel engine in cold weather.

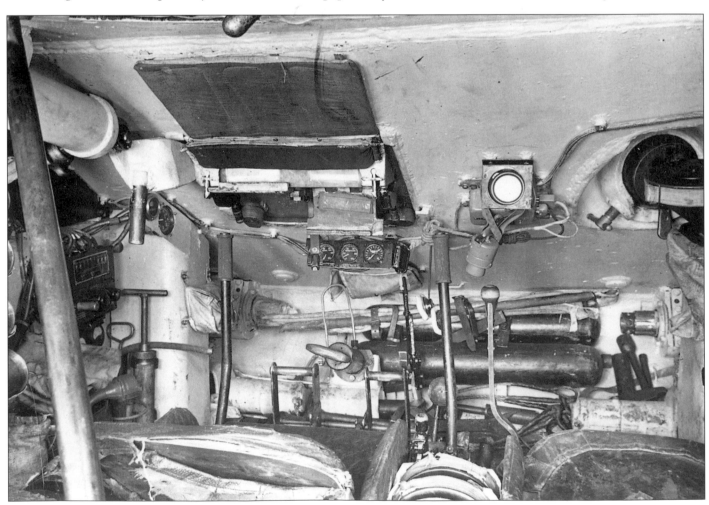

Above: A captured ex-North Korean T-34/85, showing the hull front, armoured mount of the hull machine gun, the driver's hatch, and spare track secured to the front.

greatest tank designer of a generation. He was replaced by Koshkin's deputy, Alexsandr Morozov, now head of conceptual design, and the driving force behind the work on the new transmission.

LAYOUT OF THE T-34

The layout of the T-34 was fairly conventional by the standards of World War II tanks, although rather more spartan with regard to crew comforts than Western tanks, being made up of hull and turret, engine, steering unit, transmission and the chassis and suspension.

THE CHASSIS AND SUSPENSION

The T-34's chassis was based on the tried and tested Christie system that had proved so successful on the BT series. The tank had five pairs of large road wheels with a gap between the second and third wheels. Each wheel's suspension was

independently mounted, and transversely swung on a vertical coil spring located inside the hull. The drive sprocket was mounted at the rear to reduce vulnerability. It was the same roller type used on the BTs. The drive sprockets drove wide 47.5mm (19in) skeleton-type cast manganese-steel tracks with centre guide horns on alternate track links. The system had an interesting and ingenious method of retaining its track pins. The round-headed pins were inserted from the inside; there was no retaining device used on the track itself. Instead a curved wiper plate was welded to each side of the hull at the rear, level with the top run of the track. Therefore, any loose track pin passing the wiper plate in motion was immediately knocked back into place. The method also allowed the rapid removal and replacement of track blocks, considerably easing and speeding up maintenance and repairs in the field.

The wide tracks provided a small specific ground pressure which compared very favourably to that of Western tanks. The ground pressure of the T-34 did not exceed 0.7-0.75 kg per cm^2 (10-10.6lb per in^2) as compared to British, German and American medium and heavy tanks whose ground

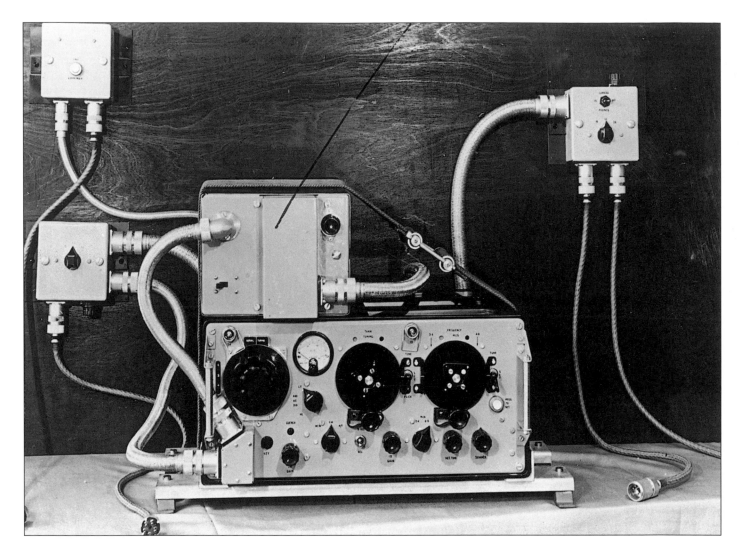

pressure was between 0.95 to 1 kg per cm² (13.1-13.9lb per in²). Track guards covered the top of the suspension system and extended 25cm (10in) beyond the hull at the front and 10cm (4in) at the rear. The combination of the Christie suspension and wide tracks worked well. The suspension

Above: Not all tanks were equipped with radios, which made coordination in battle problematic and hampered tactical effectiveness.

permitted the T-34 to retain high speeds even when moving over rough terrain, while the wide tracks on tank weighing

T-34 RADIOS

	71-TK-3	71-TK-1	9-R
Type	AM	AM	AM
Frequency (megacycles)	4–5.6	4–5.6	4–5.6
CW range (km)	48 (34 miles)	48	48
Voice range (km)	28 (17 miles)	28	24 (15 miles)
Power plant (watts)	5		
Power required (v)	12	12	12
Antenna length (m)	3.9 (4.3yds)	3.9	0.9 - 6.0 (1-6.6yds)

only 28.3 tonnes (28 tons) meant that it could traverse mud and snow that would bog down the PzKpfw IIIs and IVs. This was a useful advantage in the Soviet Union climate.

THE HULL AND ARMOUR

The hull, designed by Nikolai Kucherenko, overhung the tracks and had sloped sides. It was constructed of homogeneous rolled steel plate and electro-welded throughout using only three thicknesses of armour plate: 45mm (1.8in) front and sides; 40mm (1.6in) at the rear; and 20mm (0.8in) on the top. The standard of welding was poor, but not so bad as to allow weld failures. The glacis plate was free of apertures apart from the driver's hatch and the ball-mounted hull machine-gun. The driver's hatch also contained his periscope. The glacis plate was set back at 60 degrees and was 45mm (1.8in) thick. The sloping armour gave excellent ballistic protection and provided the equivalent protection of 75mm (3in) of vertical plate. This level of armour made the T-34 virtually invulnerable in 1941.

Below: The TPK-3 interphone system used by the T-34's crew to communicate internally. The cloth helmet contains earphones and a throat microphone.

The standard German 37mm anti-tank gun, the 50mm weapon on the PzKpfw III and the short-barrelled low-velocity gun on the PzKpfw IV were all ineffective against the T-34. The Germans often had to press the famous 88mm anti-aircraft gun or artillery into the anti-tank role. Thus the Germans were forced to hastily up-grade the guns on their two main battle tanks, produce new infantry anti-tank guns and design totally new tanks that were capable of defeating the T-34. An inspection at the British School of Tank Technology found the armour quality – although it was roughly finished – was equal or superior to British armour. As the Germans gradually began to restore the balance, some Soviet tank crews welded up to 15mm (0.6in) of extra armour plate in several places in waffle-like patterns. However, as the additional weight put extra strain on the engine and suspension, this was not adopted as standard.

The rear deck behind the turret was slightly raised to accommodate the row of engine compartment grills and engines access plate with exhaust pipes on either side. The upper rear plate and the engine cover plate were fastened with screws that could be removed if repairs on the transmission – a fairly common occurrence given the troublesome nature of the T-34's process – or engine were neces-

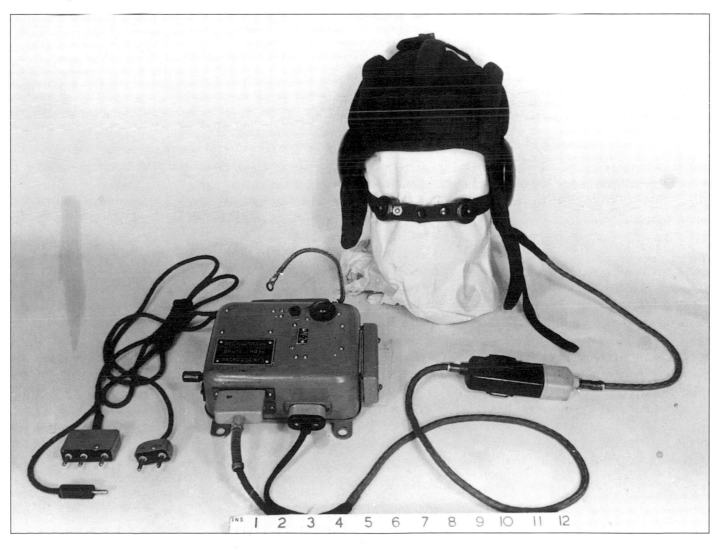

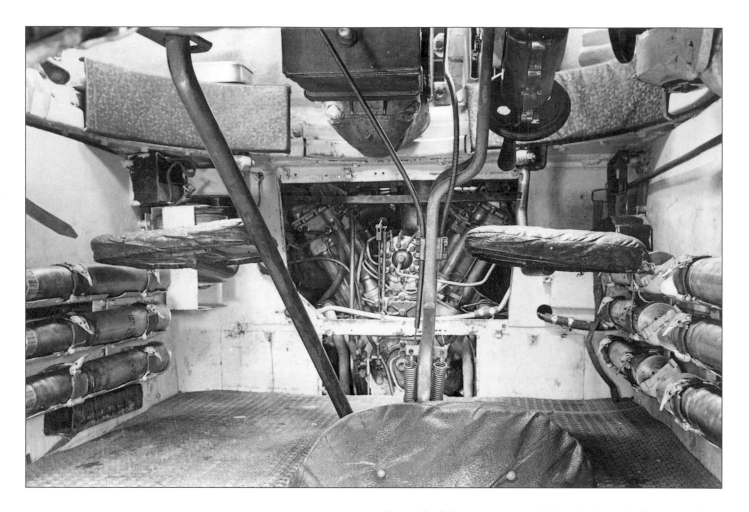

sary. On later models handle rails were fitted on the sides of hull for use by tank-borne infantry.

THE DRIVER AND HIS CONTROLS

The driving compartment was separated from the engine by the tank's single bulk head. The driver sat on the left front of the hull. He had a large one-piece hatch in front of him which hinged forward to allow access to the hull. The hatch also mounted the driver's observation periscopes. The driver steered the tank by a clutch and brake system which was controlled by two steering levels and gear change lever and a manual clutch pedal and foot brakes. The controls were linked to the transmission at the rear by metal rods running along the floor. This meant that the controls required more strength to operate than Western tanks where the transmission and gear box were close together. There was no power-assisted control gear. T-34 drivers soon learnt to keep a small mallet close to hand for use on the controls should they seize. The four-speed gear box was replaced by a five-speed type on the last T-34 Model 1943s which made it easier to change gear and increased the speed of the tank. Only 100 or so of this version were built. There was a fuel injection pedal on the floor with the clutch and brake pedals. In a foot position at the bottom of the hull was another pedal (often referred to as the Desantov) which allowed the driver to immobilise the tank even under fire. Also by the driver's feet

Above: The fighting compartment looking backwards. The commander sat in the seat, suspended from the turret ring, on the right of the picture; the loader sat to the left.

was a pair of compressed air bottles which were used to start the diesel engine in particularly cold weather. This gave the T-34 a considerable advantage in the harsh Russian winter; the Germans had to resort to lighting fires under their tanks in an effort to enable their petrol-engined vehicles to start.

THE HULL GUNNER/RADIO OPERATOR

The hull gunner/radio operator sat in the front right of the hull. He had an escape hatch in the floor in front of him. In combat he operated the Degtaryev DT 7.62mm machine-gun which was housed in a ball mount. The hull machine-gun had a 24 degree horizontal fire arc and a vertical arc of -6/+12 degrees. The Model 1942 tanks were provided with an armoured mount, no doubt much to the relief of the gunner. He was also responsible for the vehicle's radio, although early in the war it was the exception rather than the rule for a T-34 to be so equipped. Indeed, during some of the Red Army's acute manpower crises the hull gunner/radio operator position was occasionally left unfilled. As the war progressed, the proportion of radio-equipped tanks grew steadily. At the beginning of the war the company commander's tank was usually equipped with a 71-TK-3 radio and efforts were made to extend the available sets to platoon leaders. In the first two years of the conflict the Soviets also used the 71-TK-1. The situation improved with the widespread introduction of the 9-R radio in late 1942. Although technically the 9-R's range was 24km (15 miles), on the move its effective range was around 8km (5 miles).

The lack of radios was a key cause of the poor performance of Soviet tanks early in the war. As the tanks struggled to communicate adequately with one other, they had difficulty in coordinating their actions in combat. The Germans, who attached considerable importance to the universal provision of radios to their tank crews, commented on the poor tactical cooperation of Soviet tanks. In absence of radios the Soviets relied on an elaborate system of flag signals. There was even a special hatch in the main turret hatch to allow the use of flag signals even when buttoned up in combat. This proved impractical in action as the platoon commander had enough to deal with controlling his own tank and aiming its gun. Often the platoon commander would simply tell the other tanks in his unit to follow his example with all the limitations that entailed. The situation improved as radio production increased, and by the summer of 1943 all tanks were supposed to be radio-equipped. In reality the figure was around 75–80 per cent. Nonetheless this was a considerable improvement. The crew inside the tank communicated through the TPU-3 interphone system. The crews' cloth helmets contained earphones and a throat microphone.

THE TURRET

The turret on all models was low, reducing the height of the T-34. Although a low silhouette is useful in combat, the feature also restricted the depression of the main and auxiliary armament, particularly when firing on the reverse slope or at infantry at close range. The low turret also made the interior cramped as did the small size of the turret ring. Nonetheless this design policy has continued in post-war Soviet tank design. As there was no turret basket, the driving compartment led directly into the turret's fighting compartment at any position of traverse.

THE COMMANDER AND LOADER

The most serious flaw of the whole T-34 was poor ergonomic design of the turret. The turrets of the opposing German tanks had a three-man crew: a gunner; a loader; and a commander. The commander had to observe the terrain, direct the crew and coordinate the tank with the rest of the unit. The situation was somewhat different in the cramped confines of the two-man turret of the T-34. The Soviet commander had the same tasks as his German counterpart, but he also had to aim and fire the main gun, a task enough in itself and a very serious distraction from his command functions in the heat of battle. Loading was also a full-time

role and there was a brief experiment in giving the commander the job of loading the gun rather than firing it. This proved even less successful and was soon discontinued. As there was no turret basket, the turret crew sat on stools suspended from the turret ring. The commander sat to the left of the gun and the loader on the right. The loader was also responsible for the operation of the co-axial machinegun.

The T-34 aiming and vision devices were considerably poorer than those used by the Germans. The main telescopic gun sight on the earlier models was the TOD-6 and the TMFD was introduced later; both provided 2.5x magnification. During the particularly desperate fighting around Stalingrad, the T-34s from the Stalingrad tractor plant were often driven off the production line and straight into battle. These tanks lacked gun sights and could only be aimed at almost pointblank range by the loader peering down the barrel while the gunner traversed the turret. For general viewing the commander and loader both used the PT-6 periscope. Later tanks were fitted the PT-4-7 and PT-5. Wartime shortages often meant the loader's periscope was deleted. These provided a very narrow field of vision and this was not much improved by the provision of armoured viewing ports at shoulder level of both the loader and commander. There were pistol ports below these and also one in the rear, although these were sometimes omitted on later models. German tank-killing infantry were trained to make use of the T-34's copious blind spots.

Many German tank commanders liked to fight with their head out of the turret. If the T-34 commander wanted to obtain the 360 degree view afforded by this method of observation, his view was severely curtailed by the large clumsy one-piece hatch that opened forward. The only way to avoid this was to completely expose himself and sit on the turret roof, risking not only enemy fire but the extremely heavy hatch falling in his lap. Such was the size of the hatch that opening it also exposed the loader. The T-34 Model 1943 introduced separate hatches for the commander and loader, but only on the final models was a 360-degree commander's cupola fitted.

The turret itself was originally made of rolled plate with the gun in a cast contoured cradle. On the Model 1941 the cast gun-cradle was replaced by an angular bolted type. During the production run of the Model 1942 a second version entered service with a 52mm- (2in-) thick cast turret, although it virtually the same as the original rolled turret.

THE T-34M AND THE NEW HEXAGONAL TURRET

The Deputy People's Commissar for Defence and head of the Main Artillery Directorate (GAU), G.I. Kulik, disliked the T-34 and insisted various changes be made to the design. This disrupted early production and led to the Council of People's Commissars ordering an improvement programme for the T-34. This programme envisioned replacing the whole

Christie suspension system with the torsion bar system used on the KV and T-50 tanks and a complete redesign of the hull and turret with an increase in armour. The new design was called the T-34M. The project broke down when it became clear that it would seriously disrupt production. Morozov had designed a new turret for the T-34M in response to some of the flaws of the earlier turrets that had shown up in combat. The accepted practice of German tank-killing infantry squads was to climb on to the back of the tank and wedge a teller mine under the turret overhang. The overhang also created a shell trap that deflected incoming rounds into the vulnerable turret ring. Morozov's new turret which appeared on the Model 1943 eliminated the overhang. The cast hexagonal turret was also considerably easier to manufacture and larger than the original turrets, giving the turret crew a little more space. The problem of the small turret and overworked turret crew, however, was only adequately solved with the introduction of a large three-man turret on the T-34/85 which entered production in the winter of 1943.

ARMAMENT

The early T-34 Model 1940 was armed with the short 76.2mm L-11 Model 1938 rifled gun with a length of 30.5 calibres. During 1941 a very small number of T-34s were fitted with the 57mm ZIS-4 long-barrelled high velocity weapon which was intended for engaging lightly armed

vehicles at longer ranges than the 76.2mm L-11. The high velocity of this weapon compensated for the loss of calibre and the L-11 remained the standard gun on the Model 1940 production run, although it was not really up to the standard that the Soviets were seeking and the T-34 designers were not satisfied with the weapon.

Fortunately there was a better gun available, although Soviet bureaucracy and the interference of Kulik, the head of the GAU, did much to hamper its introduction. The 76mm USV-39 (ZIS-3) divisional artillery piece designed by F. Grabin was as General B.L. Vannikov, People's Commissar of Armaments, noted 'a classic gun of that time in its combat and operating qualities and its technical level and economy of production'. The tank variant of this gun considerably outclassed anything that the Germans had. However, due to Kulik's interference, its production was almost halted.

In early 1941 Kulik told Vannikov that the German Army was re-equipping with tanks of increased armour thickness that made the standard 45mm and 76mm guns in Soviet service worthless. Kulik recommended that all production of all varieties of 45mm and 76mm weapons should cease to free capabilities for the production of 107mm guns. Kulik suggested that he and Vannikov visit Grabin at the artillery plant Zavod Nr 92 in Gorki to discuss the quick design and introduction of the 107mm piece. Grabin was horrified and declared it an 'inopportune and dangerous scheme'. Nonetheless Kulik gained Stalin's support despite Vannikov's argument that he doubted Kulik's claim that German tank technology had advanced as rapidly as he claimed and that: 'If the necessity arose for increasing the armour-piercing potential of our medium calibre artillery, then the very first thing to be done would be to increase the velocity of the 76mm gun.'

There was no point in shifting to a completely new 107mm design. If German armour was so impenetrable as to require a larger calibre weapon 'It would be more expedient to take ... the 85mm anti-aircraft gun with a large muzzle velocity; it was part of standard equipment and was being manufactured in large quantities.' Though Vannikov had the benefit of hindsight when writing about the incident and, of course, when the T-34 was up-gunned it was initially with a higher velocity 76mm gun and finally with a modified version of the 85mm AA gun, there can be no doubt of the foolishness of Kulik's proposal.

Below: This picture shows the ammunition racks at the rear of a turret of a T-34/85. Even without the rounds, the space available is very limited and cramped.

Grabin and his team at Zavod Nr 92 already had a new 76.2mm gun in production. The F-32 was being fitted to the new KV heavy tank and achieved much better anti-armour performance than the T-34 Model 1940's L-11 due to its longer barrel. As Vannikov recalled: 'The 76mm ... gun which had been designed and put into production only recently, was the best gun.'

Kulik's proposal, however, was gaining momentum in spite of resistance of the directors and designers of artillery of the People's Commissariat of Armaments. They had concluded in a meeting on the 107mm gun 'that the proposal under consideration was not only inexpedient but ... even dangerous'. However, the key decision was taken at a meeting under the chairmanship of Andrei Zhdanov who would later prove such an inspirational leader during the siege of Leningrad. The meeting was full of military men who were always eager to gain bigger and better guns and the representatives of the Soviet armament industry had little opportunity to urge caution. When Vannikov spoke against the proposal claiming that 'You are tolerating disarmament in the face of approaching war', Zhdanov responded with a chilling reply: 'The dead hold back the living.' Stalin approved Kulik's recommendation and ordered the halt to production of 45mm and 76mm guns.

Thankfully the order had not yet been carried out when the Germans attacked, and it was immediately rescinded. The German invasion proved conclusively that their tanks'

ARMOUR PENETRATION OF L-11 AND F-34 GUNS
using the BR-350A round against vertical steel plate:

Armour penetration	100m (110yds)	500m (550yds)	1000m (1100yds)	2000m (2200yds)
76.2mm L/30.5 L-11	73mm (2.9in)	62mm (2.45in)	56mm (2.2in)	44mm (1.73in)
76.2mm L/41.2 F-34	88mm (3.5in)	69mm (2.8in)	61mm (2.4in)	48mm (1.88in)

armour was not so thick as to be invulnerable to the current generation of Soviet guns.

Kulik's interference explains somewhat the confused state of the Soviet armament industry at this time. By the end of 1940 a member of Grabin's team, P. Muraviev had adapted Grabin's F-32 gun for the T-34 and produced a weapon (the longer F-34 with 42 calibres) considerably superior to the L-11. Yet such was the baleful effect of Kulik's meddling that the new F-34 gun was not in production. In a move showing considerable initiative and courage, Grabin and the director of Zavod Nr 92, A. Elyan began producing the F-34 alongside the L-11 and shipped them to the Kharkov plant which was

building the T-34. The initial F-34 guns were completed in January 1941 and the first T-34s, usually classified as the T-34 Model 1941, armed with the F-34, rolled out in February 1941. They were mainly used as platoon and company commander tanks and proved very popular in combat after the German invasion due to their increased hitting power. Stalin became aware of the new version through letters sent from a number of units praising the design. So as units

Below: The ammunition drums for the secondary armament, the DT machine gun, were stored in racks at the rear of the turret (as shown here), and also in the hull near the hull gunner.

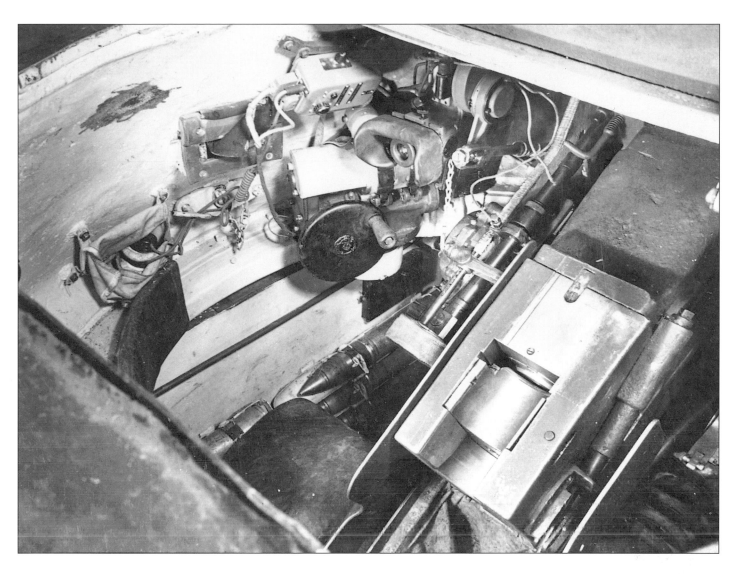

Above: A view of the turret interior of the T-34/76. The commander's position is clearly evident in the left of the picture. Note his telescopic gun sight and the main gun ammunition on the turret wall.

involved in the fighting demanded more tanks equipped with the F-34 rather than the less effective L-11, the Main Defence Committee finally authorised the F-34 in the summer of 1941. The 7.62mm F-34 Model 1940 (42-calibre length) gun equipped all subsequent models of T-34 until increases in German armour protection led to the adoption of an 85mm gun in late 1943, though tanks armed with the F-34 remained in service until the end of the war.

The F-34 had a conventional semi-automatic drop breech and the commander fired the main gun either by hand or using a foot pedal. The gun had elevation of -3 to +30 degrees. The low turret, as noted above, led to so slight a depression, while the L-11 could reach -5 degrees. The commander was responsible for turret traverse which could be done manually or electrically at a rate of 26 degrees a second. The standard Soviet armour-piercing round at the beginning of the war was the BR-350A, weighing 6.3kg (13.9lb). It was fired at a initial muzzle velocity of 655m per

second (720yds per second). In the F-34 gun, initially it was quite adequate, comfortably penetrating the PzKpfw III and capable of dealing with the latest German tank, the PzKpfw IV Ausf F, which had 50mm (2in) frontal armour at almost all ranges.

The F-34 gave the T-34 a considerable advantage in range and hitting power which the Germans scrambled to overcome. The German Mark IV Ausf H with 80mm (3.2in) frontal armour, for example, was introduced in the spring of 1943, in time for the summer campaign season. The Soviets managed to maintain their lead with the introduction of the 3kg (6.6lb) sub-calibre arrowhead discarding sabot round, the BR-350P. It could penetrate 92mm (3.7in) of armour at 500m (550yds), the average range of a tank engagement. However, the introduction of the new German tank models designed specifically to defeat the T-34 in 1943 shifted the balance drastically. The F-34 gun proved largely incapable of penetrating the frontal armour of the Tiger and Panther at normal combat ranges. At Kursk in July 1943, the T-34s were forced to close to point-blank range to engage the new German tanks on an equal footing. The only alternative was to manoeuvre to gain a shot at their side or rear. The situation

THE DEGTARYEV DT MACHINE GUN

Designer	V.A. Degtaryev
Period of manufacture	1929-44 (only in quantity after (1935)
Operating system	modified Kjellman-Friberg
Operating agent	gas
Locking system	flap on bolt unit
Feed type	drum
Capacity of feed	60
Calibre (mm)	7.62
Barrel length (mm)	1181(stock extended) (47in)
Weight (kg)	12.6 (27.7lb)
Fore sight	Guarded pillar
Rear sight	Aperture
Type of fire	automatic
Muzzle velocity (m/s)	839 (922yds/s)
Cyclic rate (rpm)	600
Effective rate of fire (rpm)	125
Effective range (m)	800 (880yds)

Below: The turret interior of a T-34/85, showing the breech of the 85mm Z15-553 gun. This 85mm gun restored the T-34's effectiveness in the face of new, more heavily armoured, German tanks.

Right: The turret interior of the T-34/76, showing the breech of the 76.2mm gun, and the co-axial DT machine gun to its right. Note the cramped turret conditions which hampered the crew.

was only resolved with the adoption of the 85mm gun in late 1943.

The T-34 carried 77 rounds of ammunition for the main 76.2mm gun. This was increased to 100 on the T-34 Model 1943. The standard combat load was 19 rounds of BR-350A armour-piercing, 53 high-explosive rounds of F-354 or OF-350 and 5 SH-350 rounds of canister. Three rounds were located on the hull side near the loader's feet for immediate use. Six more were on the wall beside the commander. The rest of the main armament ammunition was on the hull floor under the turret crews' feet, covered by neoprene matting to prevent them being accidentally kicked open. The loader had to pull back the matting before opening the bins and taking out the ammunition. The location of most of the ammunition was slightly awkward and often the hull machine-gunner would help the loader. In addition, during combat the floor would become a mess of open bins and discarded matting which would further degrade the crew's performance. The hull machine-gunner and the loader – who also manned the co-axial machine-gun – were both equipped with the 7.62mm Degtaryev DT machine-gun,

which was one of the variants of the reliable and robust 7.62mm DP machine-gun adopted by the Red Army in 1928. The DT was designed for use in tanks and armoured cars.

SECONDARY ARMAMENT

In the first 115 Model 1940 produced there was also a rear-mounted DT in the turret. The DT, a modified version of the basic Soviet infantry light machine-gun, the DP Model 1928, was to provide a weapon suitable for the secondary armament of tanks. The DT was gas operated, working on the Kjellman-Friberg system and fired at 600 rounds per minute. This was kept down to about 125 rounds per minute if the gunner wanted to avoid jamming and overheating. The DT had an effective range of about 800m (880yds). It had a retractable metal stock and wooden pistol grip and used a separate optical sight rather than the tangent leaf sight of the infantry weapon. Its magazine held 60 rounds in two tiers. The 35 drums of ammunition for the tank's two machine-guns were stored half in racks at the back of the turret, and the other half forward in the hull near the hull gunner.

CHAPTER 3

Production of the T-34

World War II was 'total war' and involved the full mobilisation of all a country's resources, including its industrial base. The war of the factories was as crucial as the war at the front.

The T-34 was an exceptionally well-designed tank and a formidable combat opponent, but what made it a war-winning weapon was the fact that it was available in such huge quantities. The German Panther was also a superb tank, but there were never enough of them available. In World War II, quality was not necessarily decisive to the outcome of battle. The scale of the struggle in the East was mind-boggling. The Red Army suffered apparently catastrophic losses and yet, much to the amazement of the Germans, remained in the field fighting as stubbornly as ever. 'The vastness of Russia devours us,' wrote Field Marshal von Rundstedt. By the summer of 1942 the Red Army had lost over two million men but still more Soviet armies appeared. On the eve of the Battle of Stalingrad, the Chief of the German General Staff, General Hadler wrote that 'At the outset of the war we reckoned on about 200 divisions. Now we have already counted 360.'

In the attritional, drawn-out conflict in Russia, the ability to equip so many formations even with so much of the Soviet Union's industrial heartland in German hands defeated the Germans as much as the improved performance of the Red Army. To quote Berte Mendeleeva, a Soviet tank school instructor: 'Who won the war? Not just our marvellous Red Army. It was the whole country, the entire population.' The stupendous effort and suffering of the Soviet population in the Great Patriotic War is well symbolised by the production of the T-34.

SOVIET INDUSTRIAL EVACUATION

The Soviet military revival of 1942–43 in which the T-34 played such a vital part was intrinsically linked to the

Left: Soviet workers put the finishing touches on a T-34 Model 1942. The Soviet Union's ability to produce the T-34 in such vast numbers was essential to the eventual Russian victory on the Eastern Front.

Above: T-34 Model 1943s and light tanks on a train. The rapid tank movement via the rail network allowed the Soviets to concentrate vast numbers of armoured vehicles for battles such as Stalingrad.

recovery of the battered Soviet industrial economy. That there was any Soviet industry left to revive was due to the remarkable evacuation of machines, equipment, and manpower that took place before the German advance. The Soviet leadership showed considerable prescience – though not Stalin, who was so shaken that he was unable to act for the first days after the invasion – by setting up a Committee of Evacuation two days after the launching of Operation Barbarossa. As the situation worsened and the key industrial centres of Riga and Minsk were lost, the State Committee for Defence ordered Voznesensky, the Chairman of the Gosplan, to draw up a plan for a 'second line of industrial defence' in the East and to organise a 'coherent productive combination between the industry already existing in the East and those transported'. The plan envisaged the evacuation of industry to the Urals, Volga, Eastern Siberia and Central Asia. Priority was given to the armaments factories.

When describing this vast undertaking, however, 'coherence' is not a word that springs immediately to mind. Engineers and workers dismantled their factories, hauled the machinery to a rail head and loaded it on to a waiting flat car. When they finally reached their destination – in for example the Urals – the workers disembarked and began to reassemble their factory. Although every effort was made to ensure the workforce stayed with their 'factory' while in transit, it was a messy, improvised affair. Workers arrived without their equipment, equipment without its workers. Nonetheless, some 1.5 million wagon loads of evacuated industrial equipment were moved eastwards with the estimated 16 million Soviet citizens necessary to man it. Between July and December 1941, 1523 enterprises, the bulk of the western Soviet Union's iron, steel and engineering plants, were moved out of reach of the German invaders.

Every effort was made to marry evacuated plants with existing factories but many industries had to set up in undeveloped areas and many of these were in the most inhospitable areas of the Soviet Union. Soviet propaganda had little need to embellish the accounts of endurance and

T-34 PRODUCTION FIGURES

| Year | GERMANY | | | | USSR | | |
	Pzkpfw II	Pzkpfw IV	Panther V	Total	T-34	T-34/85	Total
1939	206	141	-	347	c.270	-	270
1940	858	278	-	1136	2800	-	2800
1941	1703	467	-	2170	12,520	-	12,520
1942	2558	974	1768	5300	15,812	-	15,812
1943	253	3013	3749	7015	3500	11,000	14,500
1944	-	3126	459	3585	-	7650	7650
1945	-	385	-	385	-	-	0
total	5578	8384	5976		34,902	18,650	
grand total				19,938			53,552

heroism involved in the establishment of these factories in temperatures of -40 degrees and there is no reason to doubt their veracity. *Pravda* of 18 September 1942 provides a suitable example of the extremes of climate in which these feats were undertaken by the dedicated Soviet work force of the day:

The earth was like stone, frozen hard by our fierce Siberian frost. Axes and pickaxes could not break the stony soil. In the light of arc lamps people hacked at the earth all night. They blew up the stones and the frozen earth and they laid the foundations ... Their feet and hands were swollen with frost bite, but they did not leave their work.

While abandoning the workplace might well have entailed the unwelcome attention of the NKVD, the achievement of building the factory and starting production in a mere 14 days was down to more than just fear. These workers were inspired by a deep sense of patriotism and a loathing of the German invader. The example of a young woman introduced to a visiting party of Americans illustrates the motivation of much of the Russian population well. She was a prodigious overachiever in terms of production goals and was asked by the Americans why she put so much effort into her job. She simply explained that she worked from hatred of the Germans as both of her parents had died under German rule.

PRODUCTION OF THE T-34 MOVES EAST

In August 1941 the Kharkov Locomotive Plant began to be evacuated to Nizhni Tagil where it was renamed the Uralvagon Plant No 183. The new plant was married to the existing Chelyabinsk tractor works which had been switched to the production of T-34s, as was the equipment from the Kirov Plant from Leningrad. The three giant plants formed a giant tank-producing complex called 'Tankograd'. The achievements of the Kharkov works in establishing their new factory match any successes of the time, as the Official

Soviet History recalls, 'the last lot of workers of the Kharkov tank works left Kharkov on 19 October; but already on 8 December, in their new Urals surroundings, they were able to assemble their first 25 T-34 tanks which were promptly sent to the front.'

The majority of men between 18 and 50 were in uniform. The workforce, therefore, was made up of women, old men and teenagers. As Berte Mendeleeva recalled of Tankograd: 'The machinists in the workshops were mainly women and even teenagers. Some were so young that they needed to stand on boxes to reach the work bench.' They worked in appalling conditions. At one tank factory, 8000 female workers lived in holes carved out of the earth, as historian Richard Overy notes, 'in industrial bunkers that unintentionally mirrored the harsh trench conditions at the fighting front'.

THE WORKERS' HARDSHIPS

The distinction between the frontline and the rear areas, the hardships endured by soldiers and civilians, became increasingly blurred. The workers laboured 12 to 16 hours a day on rations, which were a fifth of that of the British population. On average this was merely a pound of bread and scraps of meat or fat, supplemented by whatever they could grow themselves. The endurance of the hungry, exhausted Soviet workers through month after month of backbreaking labour is staggering. To quote Overy again:

'No other population was asked to make this level of sacrifice: it is unlikely a western work force could have tolerated conditions so debilitating.'

Although the efforts of the Soviet population were awe-inspiring, much of their production achievements were down to the talents of Morozov and the T-34 design team who moved to Nizhni Tagil with the rest of the Kharkov plant. The main aim of the team was to cut costs and make production by an unskilled labour force easier. V. Buslov and

Above: A T-34 Model 1941 at a repair works. Possession of the battlefield made salvage of tanks much easier; thus as the Red Army's success grew, the more abandoned or damaged tanks it could repair.

V. Nitsenko developed a cast turret that, while similar in appearance to the welded turret, was simpler to manufacture. This was adopted on both the Model 1940 and Model 1941 T-34 which had either a cast or welded turret depending on where they were manufactured. Of the plants set up to take the slack as production at Kharkov ceased while the plant was moved east, Krasnoye Sormovo at Gorki near Moscow produced tanks with the new cast turret while the STZ Plant in Stalingrad continued to make the welded turrets.

The Model 1942, introduced in late 1941, was very similar to the previous model, apart from the fact that many of its components were simplified. For example, the F-34 gun on the Model 1941 had 861 parts, while on the Model 1942 the number was down to 614. They also managed to drive down the cost of producing the tank from 269,500 roubles in 1941 to 193,000 in 1942. Perhaps more importantly the time taken to build a T-34 was halved; the man hours involved in producing a T-34 dropped from 8000 in 1941 to 3700. Admittedly craftsmanship declined but that did not matter as the apparent crudity seems to have affected neither the protection afforded by the armour, nor the performance of the tank.

During 1942, there were serious rubber shortages in many of the plants. In response, the Stalingrad plant produced T-34s with all-metal road wheels, and other plants did the same. At high speeds, however, the all-metal wheels in contact with the all-metal track set up harmonic vibrations which were noisy and unpleasant for the crew and damaged the tank by loosening parts. As rubber became available again, rubber-rimmed wheels were used in the fifth and sixth position which caused fewer problems. By 1943, the all-metal wheels had disappeared.

In the autumn of 1942, production at Stalingrad was closed down due to the heavy fighting in the city. The production was further extended in Tankograd, and the Ural Heavy Machine Tool Factory in Sverdlovsk was converted to production of T-34s. By now the Soviets were beginning to out-produce the Germans and wear them down through a terrible war of attrition in which the Germans could never catch up.

VICTORY IN THE NUMBERS GAME

Within a few months the Germans had captured the main industrial and agricultural areas of the Soviet Union. A third of the rail network was lost; the supply of iron ore, coal and steel was cut by three quarters. A confused mass of workers fed by a considerably shrunken food supply fled with their equipment from a rapidly advancing enemy into a vast harsh hinterland on an overloaded and deteriorating transport network. Any sensible government would have given up the situation as hopeless, yet this mauled shrunken base was able to rebuild the Soviet armaments industry and equip over 200 divisions.

The recovery was remarkable. Although there was a serious drop in production as the industries were moved eastwards in 1942, the Soviet Union produced more weapons than the year before and, surprisingly more than the enemy. Many of these weapons, the T-34 in particular, were of a quality equal or better than those of the Germans. The uneven confrontation of 1941 was reversed by a combination of improved skills in the Red Army and the provision of more and better weapons. In 1943, the gap began to widen still further. That year the Soviet Union produced double the number of tanks produced by the Germans. In the crucial area of medium tanks, the Soviet were massively out-producing the Germans from 1942 onwards.

HIGH SOVIET PRODUCTION LEVELS

The Soviet economy out-produced the German economy from a far smaller resource base and with a less skilled work force. Much of this was down to the simplicity of production goals and the single-minded concentration on the production of proven types. The Soviet Union only produced two tanks in great quantity during the war compared to the plethora of models fielded by Germany (and the British and Americans). The T-34 design was mechanically simple, facilitating quantity production with limited resources in specialised machine tools and skilled labour. Also the T-34 had a great number of parts which were interchangeable with the other successful design, the KV, such as the engine, gun, transmission, and vision devices. The Soviets did not have to spend so much time in developing models because their tanks were so advanced. In response to yet another complicated and superbly engineered tank fielded by the Germans (in inadequate numbers) all the Soviets did was introduce a counter-modification to their two standard tanks. Only towards the end of the war did they introduce a new tank, the IS (Iosef Stalin), but even that was simply a redesigned KV.

It is not the KV or IS that symbolise the extreme efforts of the Soviet population in World War II; it is the T-34. It was a tank that could beat the best tanks the Germans had, but it had to be produced in thousands, in conditions of terrible hardship, to repel the Nazi invader. The workforce's sacrifice is beyond imagination. Truly in Total War, the factory is as decisive a factor in victory as the battlefield.

Below: Crews in front of factory fresh T-34 Model 1943s. Crews from the training schools attached to larger tank factories would see their tanks' construction and drive them off the production line to the front.

CHAPTER 4

Combat Performance: World War II

The presence of the T-34/76 in 1941 proved to be a rude shock for the Germans. Compared to other Soviet tanks, the T-34 was able to take on and destroy the best of the German panzers. In various modifications, and despite some setbacks, the T-34 held its own until the war's end in the ruins of Berlin in 1945.

In June 1941, when the Germans launched their invasion of the Soviet Union, Operation Barbarossa, the Russians had a total tank force of some 20,000 tanks. The huge number of Soviet tanks masked the fact that Russia had sacrificed quality for quantity, for the vast majority of these tanks were no challenge for the aggressive German panzer crews: poorly armoured, under-gunned and with minimal armour, tanks like the T-26, T-28 and the BT series quickly succumbed to the fire and tactics of the German panzers. Indeed, the life expectancy of the average T-26 was about 100 motor hours, after which they needed a major overhaul including an engine replacement.

There were, however, almost 1000 T-34/76 tanks with the Soviet forces in June 1941 and these provided quite different opposition. The T-34, with its long 76.2mm gun, quickly proved its worth. The T-34's mathematically angled hull armour which overhung the tracks gave ballistic protection twice that of the 45mm (1.77in) armour used; the sloped armour was vital for defence; the 76mm gun gave offensive firepower. In addition, the high-performance diesel engine and wide tracks gave the T-34 the mobility to match the German panzers. As has been seen, this balance of firepower, armour design and mobility was the starting point for modern tank design. In the early days of 1941, one drawback

Left: Tank-borne infantry aboard a T-34 in March 1944 during the Russian Winter Offensive. The Red Army's lack of armoured personnel carriers meant that T-34s were used to carry infantry.

Above: A T-34 (leading) and a T-26 (rear) support Soviet ski troops. The T-34's wide tracks and diesel engine, with well-equipped Soviet infantry, made a formidable winter force against the Nazi invaders.

the T-34 suffered from was insufficient ammunition. In 1941, many T-34 tanks went into action without any armour-piercing shells, only high explosive, while some tanks were without a full load of ammunition. The Russians were also handicapped by a lack of radios to coordinate their tanks in battle. These shortcomings would be remedied as the war unfolded to make the T-34 increasingly effective.

FIRST BATTLES: BRODY-DUBNO, JUNE 1941

As the German Army Group South pushed into the Soviet Union in 1941, the available T-34s proved to be a more formidable opponent than the lumbering Russian tanks that were usually encountered and which were so easily picked off by the German panzers. The first major battle between advancing German armour and T-34s came in late June 1941. General Mikhail Kirponos, commanding the Soviet Southwest Front, decided to attack the German armoured tip of Army Group South with a flanking attack thus blunting – and, he hoped, halting – the German advance.

Kirponos's target was Panzer Group One, operating ahead of the main body of Army Group South, commanded by General Ewald von Kleist, and consisting of 9th, 11th, 13th, 14th and 16th Panzer Divisions. With great difficulty, Kirponos massed his tank force, which included several hundred T-34s and heavier KV tanks. Rough terrain and

Luftwaffe strafing attacks hampered the grouping of his armour for the attack. As a result, Kirponos's tanks went into the assault piecemeal.

On 26 June, the battle of Brody-Dubno climaxed with the Soviet tank attack to cut off Panzer Group One. At this stage of the war, the training of the Soviet tank crews was poor. A post-war report by the German commander Franz Halder recalled how:

'The training of the individual tank driver was inadequate; the training period was apparently too short and losses in experienced drivers were too high. The Russian avoided driving his tank through hollows or along reverse slopes, preferring to choose a route along the crests which would give fewer driving difficulties. This practice remained unchanged even in the face of unusually high tank losses. Thus the Germans were in most cases able to bring the Russian tanks under fire at long range and to inflict losses even before the battle had begun. Slow and uncertain driving and numerous firing halts made the Russian tanks good targets.'

While training was poor for the Russian T-34 tank crews at the battle of Brody-Dubno, the actual tanks were remarkable. All the Russians needed to concentrate on were tank crew training and producing sufficient numbers of T-34s for battle. For instance, at Brody-Dubno one T-34 shrugged off 24 37mm armour-piercing rounds from German anti-tank guns, and only retired when its turret jammed with a subsequent round that had slammed into the turret. The problem for the Russians was that there were too few T-34s (and KVs) and too many older T-26s, T-28s and BTs that were rapidly destroyed by the Germans.

The battle of Brody-Dubno gave the Germans a nasty shock. The Russians assaulted General Siegfried Heinrici's 16th Panzer Division on 29 June and the Germans reeled back from the battlefield; only darkness prevented the Russians following up their success. The end of the battle, in early July, saw Kirponos withdraw what remained of his

Below: T-34 Model 1941s make their way down Leningrad's Moskovi Prospect towards the front in 1942. The 900-day Siege of Leningrad, an awesome feat of Soviet endurance, saw T-34s heavily involved.

force towards Kiev. The battle had certainly shattered Kirponos's tank force, and Kirponos himself died defending Kiev, but this early encounter was a portent of later battles where masses of T-34s with well-trained crews would take on, and defeat, the best of the German tank crews. The Brody-Dubno battle cost the Germans more tank casualties than any other encounter in 1941.

The German Panzer commander General Heinz Guderian rated highly the T-34, commenting in late 1941:

'Numerous T-34s went into action and inflicted heavy losses on the German tanks. Up to this time we had enjoyed tank superiority, but from now on the situation was reversed. The prospect of rapid, decisive victories was fading in consequence. I made a report on this situation, which for us was a new one, and sent it to the Army Group; in this report I described in plain terms the marked superiority of the T-34 to our Panzer IV and drew the relevant conclusions as they must affect our future tank production. I concluded by urging that a commission be sent immediately to my sector of the front and that it consist of representatives of the Army Ordnance Office, the Armaments Ministry, the tank designers and the firms which build the tanks ... The officers at the front were of the opinion that the T-34 should simply be copied, since this would be the quickest way of putting to rights the most unhappy situation of the German Panzer troops.'

T-34 VERSUS THE GERMAN PANZER MARK III

In July 1941, further encounters with the T-34 showed the effectiveness of this new tank. On 8 July 1941, Panzer Mark IIIs of the German 17th Panzer division saw a single Russian tank approaching whose silhouette was unfamiliar. As usual, German gunners opened fire, expecting to see the tank destroyed, only to watch their rounds ricochet off the tank's turret. Increasingly alarmed, the Germans watched this new tank shrug off the shells from their standard 37mm anti-tank gun as it advanced on its squat tracks through the German position, crushing the anti-tank gun as it went. The tank, a T-34, then disappeared behind the German positions. In the end, after a 14.5km (nine-mile) excursion behind the German lines, the Russian tank was only stopped with a shot into its rear from a 100mm gun.

Again in July 1941, a 37mm anti-tank battery of Panzerjäger Abteilung 42 reported how they had encountered 'a completely unknown type of tank ...We opened fire immediately but the armour was not penetrated until the range was 100 metres. Armour-piercing projectiles stick in the armour plating at 200 metres.' Another gun crew reported: 'Half a dozen anti-tank guns fire at the T-34, which sounds like a drum-roll. But he drives staunchly through our lines like an impregnable prehistoric monster.' Eventually, only the arrival of the PAK 40 75mm anti-tank gun could restore the balance.

T-34/85

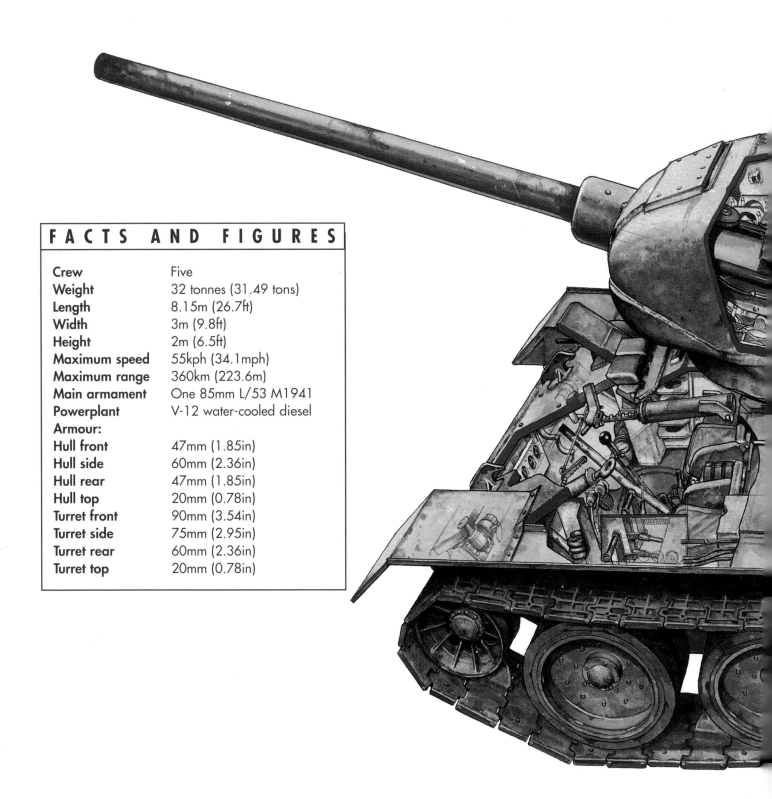

FACTS AND FIGURES

Crew	Five
Weight	32 tonnes (31.49 tons)
Length	8.15m (26.7ft)
Width	3m (9.8ft)
Height	2m (6.5ft)
Maximum speed	55kph (34.1mph)
Maximum range	360km (223.6m)
Main armament	One 85mm L/53 M1941
Powerplant	V-12 water-cooled diesel
Armour:	
Hull front	47mm (1.85in)
Hull side	60mm (2.36in)
Hull rear	47mm (1.85in)
Hull top	20mm (0.78in)
Turret front	90mm (3.54in)
Turret side	75mm (2.95in)
Turret rear	60mm (2.36in)
Turret top	20mm (0.78in)

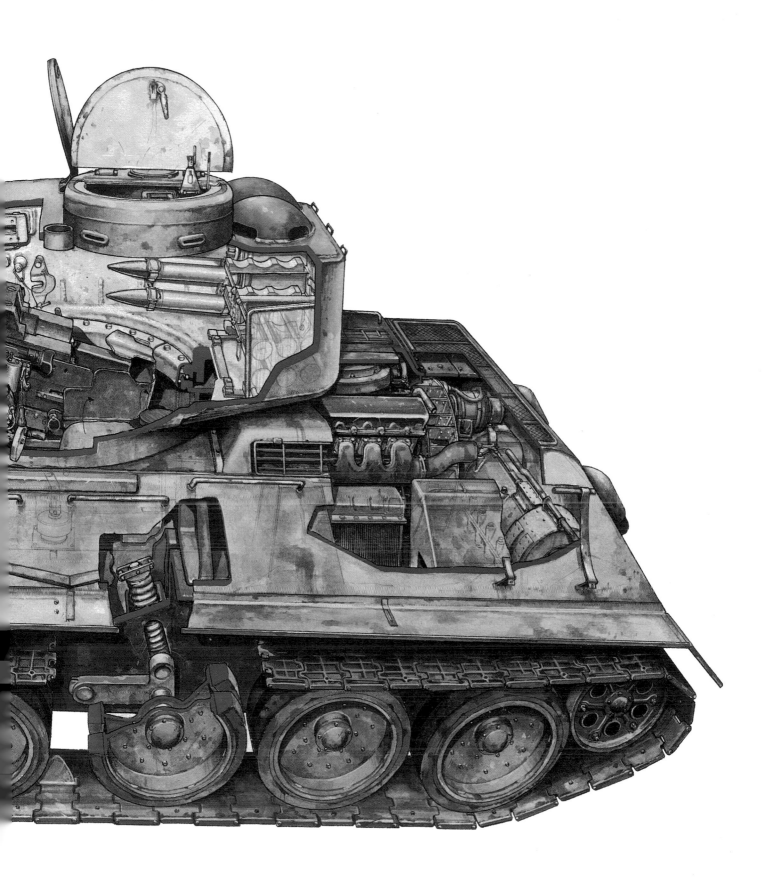

The German Mark III Panzer tank was unable to take on the T-34. One PzKpfw III crew reported: 'Quite remarkable, Lieutenant Steup's tank made hits on a T-34, once at about 20m (22yds) and four times at 50m (55yds) with the PzGr. 40 projectile without any noticeable effect ... The T-34s came nearer and nearer although they were constantly under fire. The projectiles did not penetrate but sprayed off the side.' A German tank officer from Pz.Abt.4 reported: 'Time and time again our tanks have been split right open by frontal hits. The commander's cupolas on the PzKpfw III and PzKpfw IV have been completely blown off, proof that the armour is inadequate and the attachments of the cupolas is faulty. It is also proof of the great accuracy and penetration of Russian T-34's 76.2mm gun ...The former pace and offensive spirit [of the Panzer force] will evaporate and be replaced by a feeling of inferiority, since the crews know they can be knocked out by enemy tanks while they are still a great distance away.'

PRODUCTION OF THE T-34

The T-34 shattered the confidence that German troops had in their technical superiority. Here was a tank, produced by an enemy portrayed as racially inferior, which was able to blunt anything in the German armoury. At first, the limited number of T-34s restricted their effectiveness, but once the Soviet economy geared up for war and mass-production of the T-34, the Germans would struggle to match their enemy. As the

Above: A rather spectacular picture of the fate of two T-34 Model 1941s in August 1942. The Germans had relaunched their offensive, towards Stalingrad, which resulted in high Soviet losses.

Germans saw the Russians as racially inferior, they were also unwilling to learn from their enemy and copy the design features that made the T-34 tank so effective. This would cost the Germans dearly as they tried to bring new models like the Panther and Tiger into production in time to counter the T-34.

The war on the Eastern Front was a tank war. While large infantry formations were involved, and while there was street fighting at battles like Stalingrad where tanks were of limited use, the war in Russia witnessed the biggest tank battles in history. In 1941, Russia produced around 3000 T-34s and at first the problem was finding crews to man the tanks, as so many Russians were killed or taken prisoner by the Germans in their advance following Operation Barbarossa. When the Germans had invaded, the Russians, with superhuman effort, had moved factories and workers east to escape them. From July 1941, a massive programme had transferred Russia's key factories away from the war zones. Industrial plant was dumped off railway wagons and workers rebuilt their factories to restore production. Soon great tank factories sprang up in and around the Ural Mountains, safely behind the Russian frontline, and they rapidly outpaced the Germans in the production of main battle tanks. It was not just the T-34 tanks and their crews that would win the coming battle, but, as has been seen in the earlier section on tank production, the industrial base that produced sufficient T-34s for the front.

THE T-34 AS A FIGHTING MACHINE

Unlike the German tanks it would come up against, the T-34 was not a sophisticated machine. While the original T-34s exhibited high levels of craftsmanship, the exigencies of war meant that later models were crudely built. As production increased, many of the hull fittings were simplified and some features, such as a second roof periscope for the loader, were simply omitted. The T-34 was rugged and simple, and symbolised the whole spirit of the Russian war effort. Concentrated on the three characteristics that made the tank so deadly: gun, armour and mobility. The Russian crews who manned the T-34 had none of the creature comforts expected by crews of the German panzers or Allied Shermans. But the hardy peasants (including women) who manned the T-34 were unlike the young Americans, Germans and British who were trained for tank duty. The average Russian had no experience of automobiles from before the war: theirs was an unmechanised society. Therefore, the simple layout of the T-34 suited the Russian recruit, and unaccustomed to the luxuries of a private motor car, these recruits made few complaints about the spartan interiors of their T-34s. These simplicities, as will be shown, also suited the T-34 for use after the war in Africa and Asia among emergent nations unsuited to the technical complexities of American or British tanks. On the negative side, the two-man turret of the T-34/76 was cramped and inefficient, with the commander having to

Below: Russian infantry march past a line of T-34s, probably Model 1941s. On the turret of the nearest is a typical painted patriotic slogan, an exhortation to the 'motherland', to increase morale. Such slogans were encouraged by Soviet political officers.

Above: A T-34 ablaze on the Russian steppes in late 1942 or early 1943. By late 1942, the T-34's superiority was being undermined on the Eastern Front by new German tanks such as the Tiger.

act as gunner, as well as directing the tank in battle. This hampered the T-34/76 when in action against the five-man German tanks and was remedied in the later version of the T-34, T-34/85, with a bigger, three-man turret.

THE BATTLE FOR MOSCOW, 1941

When the autumn mud descended on the Russian Front in late 1941, the remaining T-34s were still mobile as their wider tracks (48mm/19in) compared to the Panzer III (35mm/14in) allowed them to pass through the bogs of mud in which the German tanks foundered. In October, the Russian 4th Tank brigade, containing what few T-34s the Russians had at the front, launched a local counterattack. Russian tactics at this stage were crude; there was none of the specialist training of the German tank crews. Nonetheless, the German advance was blunted and 30 panzers were left burning on the Russian steppe. This engagement had been part of the German drive on Moscow, codenamed Operation Typhoon. It was imperative that the Germans captured the Russian capital before the freezing winter immobilised men and machines. For the German tanks, without proper winter equipment, it was a race against time.

Above: These three T-34s were lost in Byelorussia during the early stages of Barbarossa in July 1941. In the foreground is a Model 1940. Two German soldiers are shown peering into a Model 1941.

At this early stage of the war, the few T-34s available were invaluable in the defence of Moscow. The short-barrelled 75mm gun on the Panzer Mark IV, (the most powerful German tank then available) was no match for the long-barrelled 76.2mm main armament on the T-34. The only real way to knock out the T-34 was for the German crews to put a round through the engine grating on the T-34's rear. This was guaranteed to disable the T-34 but required a cool head in the heat of battle as sweaty, tired crews manoeuvred to get around the back of their Russian foes. In all this, the Germans were handicapped by the quality of the T-34. Unlike the BTs and T-28s encountered in the opening stages of Barbarossa, the Germans could not pick off the T-34. As a Panzer sergeant recalled: 'Numbers – they don't mean much, we were used to it. But better machines, that's terrible. You race the engine, but she responds too slowly. The Russian tanks are so agile, at close range they will climb a slope or cross a piece of swamp faster than you can traverse the turret. And through the noise and the vibration you keep hearing the clang of shot against armour. When they hit one of ours there is so often a deep, long explosion, a roar as the fuel burns, a roar too loud, thank God, to let us hear the cries of the crew ...'

The actions of small units of T-34s slowed down the German advance on Moscow as Stalin gathered his forces for a desperate defence of his capital. As the snow and ice spread, the lubricants in the German tanks froze, mechanical parts seized up, and German crews lit fires under their machines to keep the tank engines from bursting. The Russian winter proved to be an unforgettable experience for the German tank crewmen. Their vehicles, designed for European operations, were not built to withstand such extremes. The slicing winds and freezing temperatures made the track and firing pins brittle and liable to snap; hydraulic fluid froze in the main gun recoil buffers, rendering the gun useless; ammunition refused to fire; oil congealed to the consistency of treacle, and engines had to be kept running so using up precious fuel.

'General Winter' had arrived and here the Russians, accustomed as they were to the cold, had advantages. They pushed their versatile T-34 crews to make night assaults to unsettle the Germans; such attacks, while difficult to plan and execute, were terrifying for the tired German infantry who had to stumble out of dugouts to beat off the T-34s and Russian infantry pushing into their positions. As the Germans fell victim to frostbite, the T-34s tore into their lines and only the 88mm anti-aircraft gun had the hitting power to stop the T-34. Other means of knocking out the T-34 included placing a mine into the tracks or under the rear overhang of the T-34 turret. Both operations, involving considerable bravery and calm, were best executed at night.

As the German advance on Moscow faltered, the Russians planned their counter-attack. To lead the offensive to save

Moscow, Stalin chose Marshal Georgi Zhukov. Already the victor of battles with the Japanese in Manchuria in 1938–39, Zhukov would prove himself in World War II as one of the great commanders. Confident in the knowledge that the Japanese were not going to attack in Manchuria (a Soviet spy in Japan, Richard Sorge, gave the Russians vital access to the Japanese decision-making process), Zhukov brought from the Soviet Far East eight complete tank brigades, 15 rifle divisions and three cavalry divisions. It was not much but these troops would give the Soviets the edge, and on 5–6 December 1941, Zhukov's troops fell on the over-extended Germans on the edge of Moscow. Zhukov's Siberian infantry, equipped and accustomed to the harsh winter, proved more than a match for the Germans, and local successes for the Russians saved Moscow. Zhukov ordered his T-34s to push around German positions, bypassing any points of strong resistance, so as to get behind the German lines, and maximum advances of 104km (65 miles) were achieved in the December counter-attack. German panzer commander Major-General F. von Mellenthin commented on the pivotal part the T-34s played in the battle for Moscow: 'In 1941 we had nothing comparable with the T-34 with its 30mm (1.2in) maximum armour, 76mm high-velocity gun and relatively high speed with splendid cross-country performance. These tanks were not thrown into the battle in larger numbers until our spearheads were approaching Moscow; they then played a great part in saving the Russian capital.'

UPGRADING THE GERMAN TANKS

German tank crews undoubtedly had the better of their Russian counterparts when it came to training and tactics. However, with the weight of Soviet industry behind the mass-produced T-34, the Germans were unable to destroy the hardy T-34 in sufficient numbers to achieve victory. The Germans knew from their first encounter with the T-34 that they needed to modify their equipment. The technical superiority of the T-34 led to hysterical calls for German industry to build a comparable tank. Following inspections of captured T-34s, the Germans re-equipped the Panzer Mark III with the 50mm L60 main gun. But this was only a stop gap measure considering the poor performance of the Mark III compared with the T-34. Eventually it was decided to up-gun the Mark IV with the long-barrelled 75mm gun that achieved sufficiently high muzzle velocity to take on the T-34. While various modifications of the Mark IV provided the German army with its tank 'workhorse' for the entire war, the Germans also pushed on with new designs. These designs would come to fruition with the Panther, Tiger and King Tiger tanks, all of which were specifically built to fight successful tank actions with Allied tanks such as the T-34. Some of the features of the T-34, such as sloped and angled armour, were actually incorporated into tanks like the Panther, but the Germans were loath to accept the superiority of the T-34 and so went their own way with their new

tank designs. There was also a problem in copying the T-34's aluminium engine that made the Germans look to their own design. This meant that when the first Panthers arrived with frontline units in 1943, they had numerous teething troubles that reduced combat performances; the time taken to adjust the Panther to make it battleworthy was time the Germans did not have as Russian, British and American tank armies closed in on the Third Reich.

UPGRADING THE T-34

Battle performance was (indeed, still is) the ultimate determinant of the effectiveness of any weapons system. The battles in front of Moscow had shown the Russians that changes needed to be made to the T-34. As a result the T-34 went through numerous cosmetic changes as the war unfolded and the different tank factories adapted their production lines to meet changing battlefield needs. The overhang of the turret was reduced and the fuel supply was increased; the gearbox was also improved. A new style of driver's hatch was introduced, the rectangular transmission access hatch on the rear plate gave way to a circular hatch, and the engine grill was simplified. A new, wider 500mm (20in) track with a waffle pattern improved traction (vehicles with these modifications were known as the T-34 Model 1942). More importantly for the crew, extra armour was welded on to some models (spare track attached to the body of the tank was one way of quickly doing this), while later models came off the production lines with turret protection of 90mm (3.5in) of armour as standard. Having said this, a shortage of rubber at many of the T-34 production plants led to an all-steel wheel being temporarily introduced in 1942. This all-steel wheel was unpopular with tank crews as contact with the metal track at high speeds set up harmonic vibrations that were noisy and unpleasant for those inside, and could cause damage to the T-34 itself by loosening parts. With increased rubber supplies in 1943, the all-steel wheel was phased out. While in 1942, T-34 production jumped to over 5000 tanks, more radical changes needed to be made to the basic design to take into account the newer German models arriving on the Eastern Front. By 1943, the T-34 had become a much more effective fighting vehicle. The redesigned turret held a crew of three, vision was improved with the addition of a new cupola, and radios were added as standard. These changes culminated in a totally new T-34 model: the T34/85.

The modifications outlined above produced the other main variant of the T-34 tank, the T-34/85, that would continue as a fighting machine, as will be shown, well beyond World War II. The T-34-76 had a two-man turret that was cramped and inefficient. Therefore, the existing T-34 chassis was adapted to take a cast, three-man turret, and a more powerful gun. The three-man turret freed up the commander who had previously operated the main gun. The new gun in the T-34/85 was the long 85mm that was adapted, like the German 88mm, from an anti-aircraft gun. The upgunned T-34/85 was capable of firing a 9.8kg (21.5lb) round at a muzzle velocity of 780m/s (2600ft/s). This compared favourably to the German 88mm on the Tiger that fired a 10.1kg (22.25lb) shot at 797m/s (2657ft/s). The 75mm on the Panther fired a much smaller shot of 6.8kg (15lb) but compensated with a higher muzzle velocity of 920m/s (3068ft/s).

The extra armour, turret space and firepower meant an increase in weight for the T-34/85. Having said this, the design team that produced the T-34 with the long 85mm gun managed to combine the new features without reducing overall efficiency. While the weight of the T-34/85 rose from 27.3 to 32.3 tonnes (27 to 32 tons), and its range fell from 448km (280 miles) to 304km (190 miles), the T-34/85 was the most powerful tank in the Allied arsenal when it went into production in late 1943, and it was only marginally less formidable than the German Panther. The T-34/85 also used existing industrial production lines and so the new design could be produced rapidly and in great numbers for the Red Army. In 1943, of the 6000 T-34s built, only a small proportion were the T-34/85. But in 1944, 65 per cent of the new tanks rolling off from the tank factories in the Urals were the new T-34s with the 85mm gun. These new T-34s were decisive in providing a counter to the heavier German machines being produced by this time. By 1944, production of the T-34/85 dwarfed that of the T-34/76. In the end, wartime production of the T-34s of both types approached 40,000, making it the most widely produced tank of the war.

THE BATTLE OF KHARKOV, 1942

Even with the T-34, and other even heavier tanks like the KV series, coming into service, the Red Army still suffered

Below: Ammunition resupply on a T-34 Model 1943. The whole crew is shown as the main armament's 76.2mm round is passed through the driver's hatch and into ammunition bins on the hull floor.

Above: A line of T-34 Model 1943s being refuelled in the field. The provision of external fuel tanks considerably increased the T-34's range. Note the twin loader and driver's hatches on this model.

reverses because of poor organisation and tactics. The Russian army was learning 'on the job' and highly trained tank crews were at a premium. The Russian tank forces had been badly mauled in the first few months of the war, and the new T-34s and their crews needed time to acclimatise to the new tank and the new style of open, armoured warfare on the steppes of Russia.

In 1942, following the failure of the German attempt to seize Moscow, a new campaigning season opened with a Russian attack on the city of Kharkov on the Southwest Front. The consequent battle of Kharkov showed that much needed to be done to get the Russian tank crews up to scratch. General Semyan Timoshenko was ordered by Stalin to recapture the strategic city of Kharkov and in April 1942, he launched his attack. Initial success unduly spurred on the Russians who were then struck by a German counter-blow in May on their extended flank. Well-trained tank crews of Paul von Kleist's First Panzer army, themselves gathering for the German offensive towards Stalingrad, smashed into the Russian forces with two panzer divisions, one panzer-grenadier division and eight infantry divisions.

In scenes reminiscent of the early days of the war in 1941, 250,000 Russians were taken prisoner and, more importantly for the Soviet High Command (or Stavka), 14 precious tank brigades, largely made up of T-34s, were badly mauled or destroyed. The lessons of the battle of Kharkov on the Russian military were profound and proved that more training for tank crews was vital if the Soviets were going to make felt their superiority in quantity and quality of tanks. Unlike the self-motivated German troops, too many Russian soldiers and tank crews lacked the ability to think independently and make quick decisions. At Kharkov, for example, the Germans knocked out T-34s as they moved forward without any real plan. As the T-34s blundered about the battlefield and got in each other's way, or remained idle – having made an advance into the German lines – single German 88s or Mark IVs picked off scores of Russian tanks. Consequently, this was very much the era of the Panzer 'ace'. Following the battle of Kharkov, it was obvious that there was going to be a long learning curve if the Russians were to go successfully on the offensive.

THE BATTLE OF STALINGRAD, 1942

After the reverse at Kharkov, the Russians had few reserves on hand to stem the German offensive for 1942. This was a push southeastwards towards the city of Stalingrad and the oilfields of the Caucasus around Baku. In the hot summer weather, Friedrich von Paulus's Sixth Army raced forward to the River Volga and was later joined by Hermann Hoth's Fourth Panzer Army. The advance across the Russian steppes was a bleak experience for the Germans. One Battle of Stalingrad survivor recalled that it was 'easily the most desolate and mournful region of the East that came before my eyes. A barren, naked, lifeless steppe, without a bush, without a tree, for miles without a village.' The remaining T-34s were outfought and swamped in the onrush of the German assault. The German push continued to Stalingrad on the Volga.

Below: T-34 Model 1943 crews engage in tactical instruction. As the war went on the standard of training of T-34 crews improved. An increase in the number of radios improved battle coordination.

In the battle to take the city in late 1942, German armour was committed to the bitter street fighting. The nature of close-quarter fighting in built up areas (with the possibilities offered to determined infantry to get close to enemy tanks) meant that the German tanks became bogged down in the ruins of Stalingrad. Russian sappers knocked out the German tanks at close range with explosive charges and the battle for Stalingrad became an infantryman's war. The Stalingrad Tractor Plant remained open until September 1942, and so during the battle, even after German troops had reached the outskirts of Stalingrad, unpainted T-34s rolled straight off the production line and into battle. In some cases the workers who built the tanks even manned them for battle.

In November 1942, a Russian counteroffensive (codenamed 'Uranus') attacked the German flanks on the Stalingrad front and subsequently trapped over 200,000 German troops in and around the city. Finally, on 2 February 1943, von Paulus's Sixth Army, along with elements of the Fourth Panzer Army and satellite troops from Italy, Hungary and Rumania, surrendered: 91,000 men marched into captivity, of whom only 5000 would return home (in 1955). Stalingrad was a shattering psychological and material defeat for Germany and after Stalingrad the frontline rolled inexorably west rather than east.

Following the defeat at Stalingrad, the first German Panzer VI or Tigers (Mark 'E') arrived to stiffen the German line. The effect of these huge tanks armed with the 88mm gun on the

Camouflage schemes

Above: A T-34 Model 1941/42, Mtensk, October 1941. The paint scheme is a whitewash crudely applied over factory dark green. The white seldom extended to the rear of the hull or suspension.

Below: A T-34 Model 1943 of the 6th Tank Corps, 112th Tank Brigade, January 1943. This T-34 is painted in the typical whitewash over dark green finish.

Above: A T-34 Model 1941 wearing the typical Soviet green camouflage scheme. By August 1941 efforts were being made by political officers to paint political or patriotic slogans on vehicles.

Below: A T-34/76B at the Battle of Kursk in July 1943. Note the external fuel tank to the rear of the hull (there was another one on the other side of the fuselage).

Above: A T-34 laden with infantry climbs a bank. Life as a tank-borne infantryman was harsh, brutal and often very short. As this picture shows, the enemy was only one of the hazards.

against the T-34s was devastating. The German commander Halder remembered one of the first encounters between Tigers and T-34s:

'Normally, the Russian T-34s would stand in ambush at the hitherto safe distance of 1230m (1350yds) and wait for the German tanks to expose themselves upon their exit from a village. They would then take the German tanks under fire while they were still out-ranged. Until now, these tactics had proved foolproof. This time, however, the Russians had miscalculated. Instead of leaving the village, the two Tigers (from Heavy Tank Battalion 503) took up well-camouflaged positions and made full use of their longer range. Within a short time, they knocked out 16 T-34s which were sitting in open terrain and, when the others turned about, the Tigers pursued the fleeing Russians and destroyed 18 more tanks. It was observed that the 88mm armour-piercing shells had such a terrific impact that they ripped off the turrets of many T-34s and hurled them several yards. The German soldiers' immediate reaction was to coin the phrase, "The T-34 raises its hat whenever it meets a Tiger!"'

The new German tanks' performance was a great morale booster. It was experiences like these at the hands of the

new Tigers that led the Russians to up-gun and strengthen their T-34s with a bigger gun to create the T-34/85.

PREPARING FOR THE BATTLE OF KURSK, 1943: THE RUSSIANS

The campaigning season on the Eastern Front for 1943 was marked by the biggest tank battle in history: the battle of

Below: A line of T-34s awaits the order to advance; the commander in the foreground holds a flare pistol at the ready. Note also tank-borne infantry behind him with their ubiquitous PPSh-41 submachine guns.

Kursk. In an attempt to restore their prestige and regain the initiative following the defeat at Stalingrad, the Germans planned a huge tank attack on a bulge in the Russian lines around the town of Kursk. Over 6000 tanks on both sides would become involved at Kursk, thus dwarfing the battle of El Alamein (1500 tanks) or the Arab-Israeli battle of Chinese Farm in the Sinai in 1973 (2000 tanks). The German attack to nip out the Kursk bulge, codenamed 'Citadel', was soon known to Stalin via the 'Lucy' spy ring in Switzerland that had infiltrated the higher echelons of the German decision-making process and provided incredibly accurate details on German war plans. As the Russians knew that an attack on Kursk was impending, they turned the Kursk salient into an impregnable fortress. Six interlocking defensive belts were constructed to a depth of 40km (25 miles). Covering these belts of trenches, strongpoints and barbed wire were 20,000 guns, of which one-third were anti-tank weapons. There were also minefields laid to a density of 2500 anti-personnel and 2200 anti-tank mines per mile of front. Backing up these defences, the Russians amassed a huge force of fighters and bombers, and the biggest tank force ever. Into the bulge at Kursk, the Russian commanders Varutin and Rokossovsky crammed seven armies. Meanwhile, reserve forces of a tank army and two infantry armies were concentrated 240km (150 miles) behind the front. The reserve armies built additional defensive belts in front of their positions.

For the defence of the Kursk salient the Russians utilised the local civilian population. Russian civilians dug 4828km (3000 miles) of trenches, carefully criss-crossed to allow mobility for the Russian infantry. Artillery, anti-tank and machine-gun nests were sited to provide mutual support and create a 'curtain of fire' with which to meet the German attack. In all, 400,000 mines were laid, streams were dammed to make impassable flooded areas and otherwise rich, fertile farmland was turned into a gigantic obstacle course for the attacking Germans. When all the preparations were complete, 1,336,000 men, 3444 tanks, 2900 aircraft and 19,000 guns were ready for the battle of Kursk. Seventy-five per cent of all Russian armour was now located in and around Kursk.

The battle of Kursk would see the clash of Russian versus German armour on an unprecedented scale, and the majority of the Russian tank force was composed of T-34s. The new army the Russians built for Kursk was unlike the lumbering force that the Germans had encountered in 1941 and 1942. There were new Russian tank corps. These were fast-moving units of 168 tanks (later increased to 228), anti-tank battalions, Katyusha rockets and anti-aircraft artillery. Two of these corps, along with an infantry division, made up a tank army, the equivalent of a German panzer division. Organisation was finally improving.

PREPARING FOR THE BATTLE OF KURSK, 1943: THE GERMANS

On their side, the Germans deployed their new Panzer Mark Vs (Panthers) and Panzer VIs (Tigers); the Germans also

Above: A German T-34 Model 1941. Captured T-34s were pressed into service, although in small numbers, since German anti-tank gunners mistook them as Soviet-manned vehicles and opened fire on them.

fielded huge 'Ferdinand' self-propelled guns as well as the usual complement of up-gunned Panzer IVs. In all, some 900,000 Germans with 2700 fighting vehicles assembled for the battle of Kursk. The problem for the Germans was that their new generation of tanks were not fully ready for battle: teething and mechanical difficulties dogged the Panthers and Tigers and led to unwanted mechanical breakdowns. The Panther, which would develop into one of the best medium tanks of the war (to match the T-34), was simply not ready for action. The roads and tracks between the railheads and the assembly areas for Kursk became littered with Panthers that had broken down with transmission failures and engine fires. In Hoth's Fourth Panzer Army, of a possible 200 Panthers, only 40 were ready for action when battle began on 5 July 1943.

THE BATTLE OF KURSK, 1943

The German attack was pre-empted by the Russians who, having captured a German prisoner, knew exactly when the attack was coming, and so launched an artillery and air bombardment to disrupt the attack. When the Germans did eventually push forward they were met by defensive fire unlike anything previously encountered. But the Germans edged forward in the teeth of fierce Russian resistance. The Russian forward positions were manned with Punishment Battalions: men whose only hope of salvation lay in proving themselves in battle. Kursk quickly turned into a World War I battle with advances measured in yards. Mobile Russian anti-tank commandos launched suicidal attacks on German armour with petrol bombs or jamming devices before anti-tank guns tore into the German tanks from the side and rear. By 7 July, the Germans had advanced some 11.3km (seven

Above: Battened-down T-34 Model 1942s advance during the fighting around Vitebsk in 1943. Their speed and excellent cross-country performance are evident here.

miles) but at horrendous costs in men and equipment. On 12 July, the Russians launched a counter-offensive on the northern side of the Kursk salient. The Germans were forced back over the land they had so painstakingly conquered.

On the southern edge of the salient, Hoth's Fourth Panzer Army spearheaded the attack. With nine panzer divisions, including the cream of the SS panzer units (Leibstandarte, Das Reich and Totenkopf), the Germans managed an advance of almost 32km (20 miles). They made their furthest advance in the south when elements of the Leibstandarte established a bridgehead over the small Psel river. Hoth then swung the weight of his attack towards the minor rail junction at the town of Prokhorovka. This led to a decisive and remarkable armoured engagement when massed T-34s fought the Germans to a standstill.

T-34S AND THE BATTLE OF PROKHOROVKA

For the push on Prokhorovka, Hoth had more than 500 heavy Tigers and Panthers able to outgun the Soviets' T-34s. To make up their strength, the Soviets ordered up the 5th Guards Tank Army, commanded by General Pavel Rotmistrov. This necessitated a 400km (250 mile), three-day forced march to get the Guards to Prokhorovka. Harried by JU-87 Stukas armed with tank-busting cannons, Rotmistrov's Guards moved by day and night towards the front. The heat was intense, and the vast phalanx of T-34s, some 32km (20 miles) wide, was soon suffering from mechanical breakdowns and heat exhaustion. Dust covered everything. Yet despite all this, the bulk of the T-34s made the forced march, a remarkable feat considering that over long distances tanks were usually transported by rail. On 10 July, the 5th Guards arrived as an intact formation and got ready for battle.

To overcome the superior Tigers and Panthers, the T-34s were told to engage the Germans at such close range that their guns would be able to knock out the Tigers and Panthers. This was the armoured equivalent of hand-to-hand combat. The aim was to use the T-34's superior manoeuvrability to get behind and to the side of the Germans in order to exploit the weaker side and rear armour of the heavier German tanks.

On the morning of 12 July, two armies faced one another at the town of Prokhorovka. 850 Soviet tanks against 600 German tanks would fight the largest tank engagement of the war. At 0830 hours, Rotmistrov gave the codeword to attack: 'Steel, Steel' (in Russian 'Stalin'). The T-34s rolled forward over a 4.8km (three-mile) front into a head-on collision. Waves of T-34s suddenly appeared at speed attacking obliquely to the German line. This ran against all the rules of the tactical manuals for armoured warfare but deprived the heavy German tanks of the luxury of picking off their opponents at a great distance using their 88mm guns.

As the Russian official history recounted, the close proximity of the engagement gave the T-34s the advantage:

'It destroyed the enemy's ability to control his leading units and subunits. The close combat deprived the Tigers of the advantages which their powerful gun and thick armour conferred, and they were successfully shot up at close range by the T-34s. Immense numbers of tanks were mixed up all over the battlefield; there was neither time nor space to disengage and reform ranks. Fired at short range, shells penetrated front and side armour. There were frequent explosions as ammunition blew up, throwing tank turrets dozens of yards from their stricken vehicles ... On the scorched black earth, smashed tanks were blazing like torches. It was difficult to tell who was attacking and who was defending.'

Smoke and dusk soon obscured the fighting. The tanks became so interlocked that it was impossible to call up artillery or air support. The T-34s rolled up to point-blank range where their guns ripped into the sides and rears of the Tigers and Panthers. When the T-34s ran out of ammunition they were rammed into the German tanks; dismounted T-34 crews then set about destroying German tanks on foot.

By the end of the day, a day never to be repeated in the history of tank warfare, 700 tanks lay battered and broken on the battlefield. With hulls pierced and turrets ripped off the tanks the scene was remarkable. Thousands of charred or burning corpses littered this grotesque landscape. But the Russians had won for the German attack had been decisively blunted and no breakthrough was achieved. The victory owed much to the T-34 tank, but also to the determination of the Russian tank crews who took on the Germans at very close range.

AFTER THE BATTLE OF KURSK

On 15 July the attack in the south ended, and with it German hopes for a victory in 1943. After Kursk, the Germans would never launch a major offensive again. The SS divisions involved at Kursk, and which had borne the brunt of much of the fighting, were devastated. The SS units were no longer fighting units and were withdrawn from the front to recover. The T-34 had taken on and defeated the might of the German tank force. Some Panzer divisions at the end of the battle of Kursk were down to 17 tanks. The human cost of this victory was tremendous. Zhukov, not someone who was usually squeamish, visited the Kursk front after the battle and was awed by the scenes of devastation he encountered as he toured the field of battle.

Russian losses were undoubtedly very high in all these battles: at Kursk, 70,000 Russians were killed in the space of a few weeks' fighting. In total, the Fourth Panzer Army lost around 300 tanks at the battle of Prokhorovka, including 70 of the precious Tigers. While Soviet losses had totalled some 400 tanks, Russian industrial capacity was such that these losses would quickly be replaced. Also, as the Russians had been left in control of the battlefield at Kursk, they were able to salvage their lightly damaged tanks, and as they fought Kursk with only one type of tank, the T-34, spares problems were simplified. By contrast the Germans fought Kursk with five separate tanks and two assault guns which made repairs that much more complicated as each model needed specific spares.

After Kursk, Russian tank production of T-34s and heavier tanks like the JS (which replaced the KV series) outstripped anything the Germans could produce, and by 1943 and 1944 the sheer weight of numbers of Russian *matériel* began to

tell. The Russians concentrated on a minimum of variation and were producing around 2000 T-34 chassis per month, evenly divided between the T-34/76, T-34/85 and SU self-propelled gun.

CHANGING FACE OF RUSSIAN ARMOUR: T-34 IN 1944–45

Following their check at the battle of Kursk, the Germans went on the retreat. The Russian T-34 tank crews were now proving themselves as the equals of the Germans. It was a gradual process but allowed more daring operations that moved beyond infantry support to combined all-arms armoured operations. However, this was not a process that happened overnight. In 1942, it was not unusual for T-34 tank crews to receive as little as 72 hours of classroom training apart from their basic training. In December 1943, a captured T-34 crew appeared to have had little or no training: one tank commander admitted to his German captors that only a month previously he had been working in a tank factory when a proclamation from Stalin had been read out calling for those capable of driving a tank to take up the challenge and join the Red Army. Three weeks later the ex-factory worker was in battle. This was, however, increasingly the exception rather than the rule.

The T-34 tank, either in the form of the T-34/76 or the newer T-34/85, was central to most Soviet operations, either defensive or offensive. In set-piece attacks, they would follow the first wave of heavy tanks (KVs and JSs) to the objective, with infantry clinging to the tanks. Further waves of tanks, with infantry attached, would then move through the German positions to exploit any breakthrough. The emphasis in these attacks was on the T-34s firing while they moved. This stress on fire and movement meant that the T-34 crews were taught to carry on even when they were out of ammunition and to use their tanks to crush and batter the opposition if necessary.

When in a defensive role, the T-34s would be concealed behind the infantry to deal with any German tanks that broke through. In defence the T-34s would work with tank-destroyers like the SU-85 and SU-122 to create defence in depth. T-34s would work with one or two SUs to ambush German tanks. A tank hunting team would use a T-34 as mobile bait to draw the Germans on to the waiting guns of the heavier SUs engaging from a concealed position.

By 1944 not only were T-34 crews improving but so was the Soviet command structure. Improved command fed down the line to the tank crews. Men like Zhukov and Ivan Koniev built up the Red Army tank units, spearheaded by the T-34, to make them one of the most formidable armies the world had ever seen. Zhukov in particular was a real motivator of armies. An absolutely ruthless disciplinarian, Zhukov's arrival at one of the army fronts meant threats of firing squads and instant dismissals for anyone perceived to be slacking. Like the best commanders of the war, Zhukov had an eye for the battlefield and was able to handle huge bodies of men, armour, artillery and planes and to weld them into an attacking force. He knew that the success in any offensive was built around his armour and here it was the T34 – in particular the later version with the 85mm gun – that would make the difference. The broad tracks and mechanical excellence of the T-34 made the tank vital for operations on marshy ground. In the spring and autumn, only the T-34 could negotiate the mud and bogs of western Russia as the German forces were gradually pushed back across the territory they had advanced over in 1941. In 1941, six or seven Russian tanks were lost for every German one; by the autumn of 1944 the ratio was down to one-to-one.

The T-34 were used in mass offensive formations in the attacks of 1944 and 1945. More than 200 tanks would be massed on a front of less than 1.6km (one mile). Mainly T-34s, but also SUs and heavy JS tanks, they would move forward in waves following an artillery barrage. The T-34s in the second and third waves would have infantry clinging to the sides. This was not ideal as it affected the firing of the T-34's main armament, but in the absence of armoured troop carriers it was the only option available to transport the infantry so they could keep up with a mechanised advance. The infantry would dismount once they were close to the German lines, not least as determined German machine-gun fire could wreak havoc on the infantry exposed on any tank. In all this, the Russians relied on mass firepower and strength. The

Russians paid for the territory gained in blood, and casualties were frighteningly high. This helps explain why almost 30 million Soviets died during the 'Great Patriotic War'. Whereas the Russians could replace tank and manpower losses, by 1944 the German could ill-afford to lose men and machines. German factories were being totally outstripped by Soviet production. The Soviets could replace losses; the Germans could not. By the end of the war, the Russian tank factories (such as 'Tankograd') in the Urals were producing 20,000 T-34 chassis annually. Of these, over half were turned into T-34/85s, while the rest formed the basis of various other models and variants including self-propelled guns. World War II was very much a war of economies and Germany was simply being out-produced. Not just the Soviet Union, but America and Britain mobilised war economies that added to Germany's plight when it came to fighting 'total war'.

Russian tank and infantry units also lived off the land in a manner that was impossible for the Germans with their extensive and sophisticated supply lines. The commander of the Gross Deutschland division, one of Germany's élite formations, recalled the advancing Russian armies as totally

Below: T-34/85s advance through a liberated town towards the end of World War II. The ever-present tank-borne infantry are much in evidence in this picture.

Above: Soviet infantry with an anti-tank rifle in support of a massed T-34/76 attack in 1944. By then, Soviet anti-rank rifles were all but useless compared to enemy anti-tank rockets.

self-sufficient: all they needed was fuel and ammunition. The soldiers lived off the land, and while this led to supplies being taken from the civilian population, it gave the Soviet forces a mobility and freedom unknown with the German army.

THE BATTLE FOR POLAND

On 22 June 1944, the third anniversary of Operation Barbarossa, T-34s spearheaded a huge attack on the German lines that pushed the Germans back 720km (450 miles) and destroyed 25 German divisions. This advance proved how much Russian armour had improved in both tactics and standard of equipment. In the June 1944 attack, the Russians had sufficient armour to build huge tank armies that dwarfed anything the Germans could put into the field. The Germans were now outnumbered three to one: the tables were finally turning from the heady days of 1941 when the Wehrmacht smashed into Russia and drove to the gates of Moscow.

It was supply difficulties that halted the Russian offensive in the summer of 1944 rather than any real opposition. The Russians were now established in Poland and East Prussia, the heartland of German militarism, and stood poised to move into Germany itself. The remaining German panzers fought with tenacity and courage, but sheer weight of numbers overwhelmed them. When the Russian advance stabilised along the line of Vistula river, the Germans

attempted to shore up their front to meet the next Russian attack.

To make matters worse for Germany, Romania, allied to Germany, fell out of the war. Russian troops of Malinovsky's Second Ukrainian Front struck out to take advantage of Romania's collapse, and spearheaded by T-34s of Kravchenko's Sixth Tank Army, Bucharest was taken in September 1944. More importantly, these T-34s also captured the Ploesti oilfields, one of Germany's last remaining sources of crude oil. Soon German fighters would be grounded and the panzers stalled by the lack of fuel.

THE BATTLE FOR GERMANY

It would be Zhukov who would command the strike on the German heartland. By October 1944, the plans for a new offensive were well-advanced and 13 mechanised corps were established. These corps were made up of T-34s, leavened with some heavy tank units of JS tanks. The Russians also mobilised the élite Guards Tank Armies, reminiscent of the days of the old Tsarist armies, to smash through the German lines.

In January the thunder of Russian artillery marked the attack across the Vistula. Once the German lines had been punctured, the T-34s raced through the gap to exploit the breakthrough and push deep behind the German lines. Some T-34s were equipped with a rudimentary form of Schnorkel gear that allowed amphibious crossings, and this allowed them to pass river obstacles such as the Vistula in the 1944 offensives. To work with the Schnorkel, the T-34's turret and hull components were sealed and a long breathing tube was provided that would clear the water and provide air for the engine and crew compartments.

Wearily, the Germans fell back. Warsaw, the capital of Poland, soon fell to the tanks of the Red Army that were now advancing at a rate of 80km (50 miles) a day. However, Berlin was not taken in this advance. The halt by the Russian Army before Berlin has been the subject of hot debate: not until April 1945 was the advance on Berlin resumed. One explanation for the halt in the Russian tanks was the need to bring the logistical train forward to supply the men and tanks. Fuel was short and ammunition was needed to replenish the tanks and guns. Mechanical breakdown of the usually reliable T-34s also cut down on Soviet effectiveness as the rapid advances took their toll on the Russian tanks. There was also the question of the increasingly desperate German resistance in front of their capital. Units of every type, including Volkssturm units composed of the very old and very young, fought to halt the Soviet push on Berlin. German troops in Pomerania to the north also threatened any advance on Berlin with an attack into the Russians' flank. As with the capture of Bucharest, T-34s had to be rushed north to clear the Baltic coast of German troops. All this meant the early capture of Berlin was impossible.

THE BATTLE FOR BERLIN

By early April 1945, Zhukov's T-34s were ready for the final push. Planning was now complete for the final battle and the assaulting troops were prepared. It was a race to ensure that the Soviets, and not the British and Americans advancing from the west, captured Berlin. The attack on Berlin involved not only breaking the German lines centred on the Seelow Heights in front of Berlin, but also advancing into a built-up area encompassing hundreds of square miles of buildings, roads, sewers, tunnels and railways. As was proved at Stalingrad, tanks were very vulnerable in city, fighting where determined infantry could hold up an armoured advance using roofs, windows and sewers to enfilade the tanks with petrol bombs, mines and Panzerfausts. At close ranges and in the deadly environment of close-quarter fighting in built-up areas like Berlin, the T-34s needed to be wary.

On 16 April searchlights illuminated the German positions for the pre-dawn attack on the Seelow Heights. Artillery and fighter bombers pounded the Germans in preparation for the assault. As the tanks moved forward there was mayhem as tanks and infantry were caught by the determined German defence. Even at this late stage of the war, when defeat was almost inevitable, the Germans still fought with fanatical determination. Eventually the sheer weight of numbers forced the Germans off the Seelow Heights, but only after both sides had suffered very heavy casualties. The battle for Berlin was going to be one of the hardest fought battles of the Eastern Front. Desperately, the Germans resisted but inexorably they were pushed back into the suburbs and centre of Berlin. Pounded as Berlin was by Allied

Above: Although T-34 production ended in 1944, the tank remained in service until the end of the war. Here, a pair of T-34 Model 1943s advance through Leipzig in Germany in June 1945.

air forces during the war, the destruction was compounded by the Russians as they advanced into the city with heavy artillery barrages. The rubble provided an excellent defence from which small, isolated German units held out.

The defence offered by the German Panzergrenadier Division Brandenburg against the Soviet assault gives some idea of the type of fighting at the battle of the Seelow Heights. The Panzer Grenadiers were quickly involved in ferocious fighting as they attempted to stem the Russian onrush. These were the last days of the Reich, but this only stiffened the Germans' resolve. The Russians soon had their armour across the Oder and Neisse rivers and in the town of Kaltwasser the Panzer Grenadiers made a stand. As at Stalingrad, tanks were at a disadvantage in urban warfare, and using Panzerfausts the Germans quickly knocked out a number of the T-34s. In towns like Kaltwasser the Germans fought vigorous rearguard actions. Tank-busting teams, often comprised of Hitler Youth members, used Panzerfausts and explosive charges to take on the T-34s and JS tanks. The T-34s were accompanied in the towns by teams of Russian infantry, so the German infantry had to contend with holding off the infantry while squads moved in to lay hollow explosive charges that could disable the Russian armour. Frequently, the only weapon available was the 'Molotov cocktail' petrol bomb that could set a T-34 ablaze with a good shot. In the end, however, the Germans were outnumbered and they fell back to fight a last desperate defence of the German capital.

To overcome the German defences inside of Berlin, the T-34s often took the expedient measure of driving through the buildings to avoid exposing themselves to the German infantry waiting in the rubble of the streets of Berlin. Civilian casualties were heavy as the Russians applied overwhelming firepower to their advance. Office and apartment blocks came crashing down as the Russians pushed on to Hitler's bunker. By 27 April, T-34s and accompanying infantry had reached Potsdamer Platz, just a few hundred yards from Hitler's bunker. The last days of Hitler's thousand-year Reich were being played out in the ruins of Berlin. On 30 April Hitler committed suicide. The German Reich had lasted 12 years and had left Germany destroyed and occupied. The war on the Eastern Front was over. The war for the T-34, however, was far from finished as this versatile tank would now be employed across the globe in the wars that sprang up after 1945 as decolonisation and the Cold War took hold.

THE T-34 ON THE EASTERN FRONT

The Eastern Front was a war of armour. Had Mikail Koshkin's design for the T-34 still been on the drawing board when the Germans invaded in 1941, Russia's prospects for battlefield survival would have been slender. Had production started even a year later than it did, commanders like Zhukov and Koniev would have been without the T-34s and SU tanks that allowed them first to halt, and then push back the German

Below: 9 May 1945 – Victory Parade in Red Square. The T-34/85s and massed ranks of SU-122 tank destroyers that played such an important part in the Soviet triumph advance in formation.

attack. The mass of T-34s that rolled through the German lines from 1943 spelt the end of the Third Reich. The crews of these tanks – peasants, factory workers and clerks – became the commanders, drivers, loaders and gunners sitting inside a steel box with the prospect of a grizzly death should they be unable to escape from a tank 'brewing up' after a hit from a German '88'. The training schools and instructors turned these civilians into T-34 crews capable of taking on the élite, black-uniformed German tank crews. Behind all this lay the infrastructure necessary for armoured battle: the workshops, breakdown units, mechanics and communication networks. The Soviets were able to create the team that won the war – the tank, the crews and the backup – and the determination to see it through to the bitter end in the battle for Berlin.

The German Commander-in-Chief, von Rundstedt remembered how the T-34 tank was the 'finest medium tank in the world'. By the time the war ended, the T-34 (and heavier KV/JS) series of tanks became the starting points for post-war Soviet tank designs. They had proved themselves as efficient and battleworthy. Soviet design teams had produced a tank in the T-34 that would form the basis for tank design in other countries as well as the USSR. As the British military historian and theorist Basil Liddell Hart noted, tanks like the T-34 were 'rough, inside and out – they were not even painted. Their design showed little regard for the comfort of the crew. They lacked the refinements and instruments that Western tank experts considered necessary as aids to driving, shooting and control. Until 1943 they had radio only in the commanders' tanks ... On the other hand, they had a good thickness and shape of armour, a powerful gun, high speed and reliability – the four essential elements. The comfort of the crew was of less importance, especially as Russian soldiers were tougher than others. Regard for comfort and the desire for more instrumental aids involve added weight and complications of manufacture. Such devices have repeatedly delayed the development and spoilt the performance of our tanks. So they did with the Germans, where production suffered from the search for technical perfection ... The principles on which the Russians worked in their mechanisation programme can be clearly discerned. They picked up ideas from many different tank types abroad, and picked out features which they thought worth incorporating in their own tanks, and then developed the amalgam in a model on their own lines. They concentrated on the mass-production of only one or two types.'

American tests of a T-34 on their Aberdeen Proving Grounds confirmed Liddell Hart's assessment: 'In summing up, the T-34 tank appears to be a good design and proves adequate for mass-production and the employment of unskilled labour ... Outstanding features of the T-34 are: it is low, streamlined, powerful, of simple construction, possessing a small unit ground pressure, and great angular inclination of the armour – providing excellent all-round protection.'

CHAPTER 5

Combat Performance: Post-1945

After World War II, the T-34 continued in service, especially in Africa and Asia. From the deserts of the Middle East to the jungles of Africa, the obsolescent T-34 still gave valuable service.

Many of the tanks of World War II saw service after 1945. American Shermans were even upgraded as 'Super' Shermans and so saw extensive service into the 1960s, notably with the Israeli army. German panzers also found their way to war zones such as the Middle East where new conflicts gave these vintage tanks new purpose. However, World War II tanks were no match for a new generation of post-war tanks and the Soviets realised that the T-34, even with an 85mm gun, could not challenge new British and American tanks like the Centurion and M-26. Therefore, using the T-44 as a model, the T-54 was developed as the Soviets' main battle tank in 1946-47, with a 100mm gun. Nonetheless, the T-34 still proved itself useful as a subsidiary weapon working alongside the new tanks like the T-54 (and then the T-62 in the 1960s) in the Soviets' arsenal.

The T-34 was not only widely used in post-war conflicts inside and outside Europe, but continued in service as a battle tank in the service of Soviet-supplied armies until the 1990s. The T-34 was easy and cheap to maintain, and its long service history was remarkable compared to other World War II tanks. This says much about the usefulness of the T-34. In its post-war role, it was the T-34/85 that was employed as the T-34/76 did not have the firepower to operate on the modern battlefield.

THE T-34 IN EASTERN EUROPE

In 1945 Russian armies had swept into eastern Europe and occupied Poland, Bulgaria, Rumania, Hungary, Czechoslovakia, East Germany and eastern Austria. This occupation marked the beginnings of Soviet rule that would continue until the

Left: An Egyptian T-34 heading into battle against the advancing Israelis in the Sinai in October 1956. As its hatches are open, this T-34 is obviously still some way from the battle front.

late 1980s and the collapse of Communism. In 1953 in East Germany and Poland, in 1956 in Hungary, in 1968 in Czechoslovakia and in the 1980s in Poland there were popular uprisings against Soviet rule, and in the suppression of the 1953 and 1956 uprisings T-34s were deployed.

In June 1953 in East Germany and Poland there were revolts against Soviet rule. In the Soviet sector of Germany, and in particular in East Berlin, young Germans took to the streets to protest at the lack of democracy and oppressive Soviet control; two weeks later discontent then broke out in Poland. In putting down these revolts, the Soviets used troops and tanks, including the T-34. These two disturbances were, however, minor compared to the Hungarian uprising of October 1956. To suppress the trouble in Hungary, the Soviets again deployed T-34s, but in the serious fighting in the Hungarian capital, Budapest, in which thousands were killed, the T-34s became bogged down in bitter street fighting. The Soviets had forgotten the lessons of World War II, where fighting in cities like Stalingrad and Berlin had proved that tanks were vulnerable in built-up areas, and needed close infantry support. The Hungarian insurgents in 1956 proved adept at restricting the tanks' movements in the narrow confines of Budapest. The Hungarian insurgents lowered live tramway cables into the paths of the advancing T-34s, tramcars were used as barricades, dummy 'mines' in the form of upturned soup plates or pan lids were laid to obstruct the Russian tanks, and liquid soap was spread over the cobbles of the streets of Budapest so the T-34s' steel tracks spun uselessly. Then, while tank commanders were

Above: T-34/85s parade through Berlin as part of the East German May Day parade of 1958. T-34s like these were involved in suppressing the anti-Soviet rioting in East Germany in 1953.

kept pinned inside their cupolas by sniper fire, Molotov cocktail petrol bombs would be thrown from the top windows of surrounding buildings to set the tanks ablaze. Using these tactics the Hungarian insurgents knocked out some 40 Russian tanks.

THE KOREAN WAR

Outside Europe, the two main theatres of operation where T-34/85s were deployed for conventional battle were during the Korean War and in the Arab–Israeli conflict. The Korean War saw the first encounter between American and Soviet tanks. In June 1950, 100,000 Communist North Korean troops attacked South Korea. The South Korean capital, Seoul, was captured on 28 June and North Korean troops pushed south to expel the remaining enemy troops from the peninsula. Spearheading this advance were some 150 Soviet-supplied T-34/85s of the North Korean Army. T-34s of the North Korean 105th brigade formed the van of the attack. With three regiments of 40 T-34 tanks apiece, the 105th brigade had been formed in Sa-dong in 1947 as the 115th Tank regiment, changing into the 105th brigade in May 1949. This T-34 unit was the élite unit of the North Korean Army, and given the nickname 'The Tiger's Cave Sadong Unit'. Using the T-34s of the 105th armoured brigade, the North Koreans had managed to break the South Korean Army.

However, rapid support of the South Korean Army by the Americans (led by General Douglas MacArthur) brought these T-34s up against American armour as the Americans attempted to roll back the North Korean advance. To combat the T-34s, the Americans had the M-26 Pershing, armed with a 90mm gun, and World War II Shermans. At first, the T-34s met little real opposition. The South Korean Army was poorly equipped and the T-34/85s swept all before them. The first encounter between the Americans and North Korean T-34s involved lighter M-24s ('Chaffees') of the American 24th Infantry division. In July 1950 three M-24s fought a delaying action against a powerful force of T-34/85s. In an unequal contest, two M-24s were lost, but not before knocking out one T-34. These early encounters were salutary for the Americans, and left them with the uneasy feeling that the T-34 was impervious to their weapons.

The M-26 Pershing was underpowered for the hilly terrain of the Korean peninsula, and at first the Americans had to rely on their Shermans to counter the T-34s. But improvements to the M-26 and the Shermans (M4A3) gradually gave the Americans the edge. In a series of engagements at Obangni Ridge and in a valley near Taegu known as the 'Bowling Alley', large numbers of T-34s were destroyed by ground-attack aircraft, the fire of M-26 tanks and 89mm rockets. This engagement re-established American confidence and shattered the legend of T-34 invincibility. By the end of the war, superior American tanks were proving themselves

against the T-34 which was shown to be less than formidable against determined opposition using the latest designs of tank.

THE 1956 ARAB–ISRAELI WAR

The Korean War had shown that the T-34 was effective against weak opposition. Faced with the latest range of Western tanks in the hands of well-trained tank crews, the T-34 was becoming obsolescent. This was nowhere more evident than in the Middle East where Israel clashed with its Arab neighbours in a series of wars. The Arab states were equipped with Soviet arms, including the T-34 tank. The first clash between the T-34 and the British, American and French tanks of the Israeli Defence Force (IDF) came in the Arab–Israeli War of 1956. Tension between Israel and the Egyptian leader Gamal Abdul Nasser increased during 1956, and in October 1956 flared into open war with an Israeli invasion of the Sinai peninsula.

In the 1956 war, the IDF was equipped with conventional Shermans (a variety of models including the M4A1 and M4A2), up-gunned 'Super' Shermans, Shermans with French FL10 turrets (similar to those used on the French AMX-13) and French AMX-13 light tanks. Meanwhile, the Egyptians fielded a range of armour including Shermans and Centurions (and older British tanks like the average Valentine), but the majority of the Egyptian armour was composed of 230 T-34/85s. These T-34s were supplied by Czechoslovakia and in addition to the T-34s, Czechoslovakia also sent some JS3s, 200 BTR-152 armoured troop carriers, and 100 SU-100 self-propelled guns. In the tank battles in the Sinai in 1956, the Egyptian armour was totally outclassed by

Below: The aftermath of an Israeli air strike on Egyptian armour, including a T-34 in the foreground, retreating through the Mitla Pass in Sinai in 1956 during the Israeli–Egyptian War.

the Israelis. It was not just a question of superior Israeli equipment but also better training, motivation and tactics. In their attack to take the Sinai, the Israelis knocked out 26 T-34/85s, one T-34 command tank, six SU-100s, 40 Sherman Mk 3s and 12 MS/FL10s, 15 Valentines, 40 Archers and 60 BTR-152s. Egyptian tanks, fighting a desperate rearguard action as they retreated to the Suez canal, were not only knocked out by Israeli tanks, but suffered badly from Israeli air strikes that badly mauled the T-34s and SU-100s exposed in the open Sinai desert.

During the 1956 war, British and French forces invaded Egypt in conjunction with the Israeli attack. An Anglo-French amphibious and air assault on Port Said, at the northern end of the Suez canal, was followed by a push by British and French forces down the canal. The Anglo-French force soon came into contact with Egyptian forces defending the area. Wary of the effect that heavy tanks like the JS3 could have on their force, in the end the only armoured engagement for the British came with SU-100 tanks when British paratroopers knocked out four of them belonging to the Egyptian 53rd Artillery battery on 5 November.

THE 1967 'SIX-DAY' WAR

When the next Arab–Israeli War erupted in June 1967 (the famous 'Six-Day' War), T-34s were still being employed by the Arab armies. The 1967 war saw Israel fighting Egypt, Syria and Jordan, and both Egypt and Syria still had large numbers of T-34/85s. While newer T-54s were being absorbed into the Egyptian and Syrian armies, the T-34/85 remained a mainstay of the armoured forces of Israel's Arab foes. In the Sinai peninsula along the Egyptian–Israeli border, the Egyptian 7th

Infantry Division defending Rafah had 100 T-34/85s and JS3s; the important junction at Abu Agheila was held by the 2nd Infantry Division with 100 T-34/85s and T-54s; the 3rd Infantry Division stationed near Djebel Libni had a further 100 T-34/85s and T-54s; and the 6th Mechanised Division to the south was also equipped with a mix of T-34/85s and T-54s. In total, Egypt had over 300 T-34/85s. Over 20 years after the T-34 had rolled into the ruins of Berlin, it was still being deployed for new tank battles, this time in the deserts of the Middle East. The Israeli tank force for the 'Six-Day' War was much improved on the 1956 war: up-gunned Centurions, M-48 'Pattons', Shermans and AMX-13s; and crews were also better trained and had the experience of the 1956 war under their belts. This would show itself in the 'Six-Day' War when Israeli forces, in the space of five-and-a-half days, routed three Arab armies.

When the war stared on 5 June 1967, an Israeli offensive tore through the Egyptian defensive positions in the Sinai. A pre-emptive strike by Israeli warplanes had destroyed the Arab air force on the ground and this left the Arab ground forces bereft of top cover. The 1967 war was the T-34's last experience of real tank warfare. In the 1967 war, the Israeli tanks made short shrift of the JS-3s and the more modern T-54s. Therefore, the older T-34s provided little opposition for the Israelis. Israeli M-48 'Pattons' and Centurions quickly knocked out Arab T-34s, and in the mobile warfare of the Sinai the Israelis advanced rapidly to the Suez canal, brushing

Below: US infantry during the Korean War advance past a knocked-out North Korean T-34. For the North Koreans and Chinese, it was the main battle tank during the war, but weaker than the latest US tanks.

Above: Cuban-manned T-34s on the streets of the Angolan provincial capital of Huambo. These T-34s supported the MPLA, and proved decisive in the fighting against UNITA troops opposed to the MPLA.

aside the T-34s and T-54s of the Egyptian army. The Egyptian armour was exposed in the daylight hours to Israeli air strikes and failed to use their tanks' infra-red searchlights to fight the Israelis at night. In the fighting in the Sinai, Egyptian losses were heavy: of the 935 Egyptian tanks that had started the war, 820 had been lost by the end of hostilities (291 T-54s, 82 T-55s, 251 T-34/85s, 72 JS 3s, 51 SU-100s, 29 PT-76s, and some 50 Shermans and M4/FL10s). Israeli losses were some 122 tanks, many of which could be repaired as the Israelis controlled the battlefield.

On the Golan front between the Israelis and Syrians, the aged T-34 again proved to be no match for the modern Israeli armour. The Syrian armoured force defending the Golan Heights consisted of the 14th and 44th Armour Brigades and was made up of Panzer IVs, T-34s, T-54s and SU-100s. On 9 June the Israelis assaulted the Syrian positions, and while there was none of the large-scale tank engagements of the Sinai front, the Israelis lost many tanks in taking the hilly Golan Heights from the Syrians. Syrian losses were 73 T-34/85s, PzKpfw IVs and T-54s, seven SU-100s and some old StuG IIIs.

THE WAR OF ATTRITION AND THE 1973 ARAB–ISRAELI WAR

After 1967, the remaining T-34s in the Arab armoury were withdrawn from frontline units. However, the T-34 was still employed in a static defence role as armoured strongpoints. The T-34 was dug in and the gun provided a moveable platform for area defence. Both Syria and Egypt employed T-34s in this role: Egypt along the Suez canal facing the Israeli 'Bar-Lev' line; and Syria in her defences on the Golan Heights and in front of Damascus. In addition, some T-34/85s were converted into improvised self-propelled guns by mounting

the new 122mm D-30 howitzer in place of the turret. In both roles the T-34 saw action in the 1969–70 War of Attrition and in the 1973 Arab–Israeli War, particularly on the Syrian front where static T-34s were dug in and used to defend the road to Damascus against the Israeli push of October 1973.

THE T-34 IN AFRICA

The T-34/85 also saw action during and after the decolonisation struggles post-1945 in Africa and Asia. In Angola in 1975, the Marxist MPLA were involved in a civil war with rival UNITA and FNLA forces following the departure of the Portuguese colonial authorities. On the verge of losing this struggle, the MPLA called for aid and in November 1975 the first contingent of Cuban troops (in Soviet transport planes) arrived to help them in their struggle to retain power. The Cuban force included 90 T-34/85s (also some T-54s and 122mm rocket launchers) and proved decisive in the battles with the UNITA and FNLA rivals of the MPLA. The African bush of Angola proved to be a new environment for the T-34, but one in which the presence of a limited number of T-34s tipped the balance. By 1975, the T-34 was totally outdated as a battle tank but in the small wars that sprung up across Africa, and which did not involve large clashes of armour, the T-34 proved itself time and time again.

THE T-34 TODAY

Today, those T-34s that remain are confined to tank museums: relics of past glories. That the T-34 could still be useful in a war environment was shown in the conflict in former Yugoslavia in the 1990s where, in the bitter fighting in Bosnia, antiquated T-34s were again deployed. It is unlikely that the T-34 will ever again be used in anger but its war record and long service do justice to the remark of the German commander, General Ewald von Kleist: 'The finest tank in the world.'

V682.

CHAPTER 6

T-34: Models and Variants

The T-34 chassis provided a versatile base for various successful 'SU' tank destroyers. In addition, the T-34 was adapted to undertake specialist combat roles: flamethrower, bridge builder, mineclearer, and battlefield tank recovery.

As the T-34 was produced from different factories, models and types varied. The list below outlines the main models of the T-34 as a battle tank, and then specialist variants (such as mine-clearing, bridge-laying, flamethrower and assault gun) are examined. It should be remembered that this description is not exhaustive considering the minor variations completed by the different T-34 tank factories.

In August 1939, the Soviet Main Military Council accepted the T-34 as the Red Army's medium battle tank. The new design was completed during December 1939 and became known as the T-34 (Model 1940). On 19 December 1939, the drawings and models of the new T-34 were submitted to the High Command which accepted them for production even though the prototype had not yet been finished.

The first two prototypes were sent for use in the Russo-Finnish War in March 1940 against the Finnish Mannerheim Line but arrived too late to see combat action. The first production line models were fitted with V-2 diesel engines but shortages meant that some of these early models were equipped with the older M-17 petrol engine. Problems with transmissions (a recurring problem in tanks) were such that the T-34/76 (Model 40) often went into battle with spare transmission units secured to the engine compartment deck by steel cables. The salutary experience of the Russo-Finnish War, where the Soviet Army performed badly, forced them to speed up production of the new T-34. The Germans were unaware of this increased output of T-34s and German handbook and tank recognition material on the Red Army, published in 1941, contained nothing on the T-34. Therefore, manual supplements were quickly published following

Left: An SU-122 assault gun captured by the Germans and on display. The lack of a turret let the Soviets mount heavy calibre guns like the 122mm gun on a T-34 chassis to tackle heavy tanks like the Tiger.

Operation Barbarossa. Even then, the supplements confused the KV heavy tank with T-34 medium tank.

The Model 40 had a rolled plate turret and a short 76.2mm L/30.3 (L-11) Model 1938 tank gun mounted in a distinctive, cast cradle welded to a flush outside mantle. The first 115 models off the production line were equipped with a ball-mounted DT machine-gun in the turret rear. Later models dispensed with the rear turret machine-gun. The Model 40 established a standardisation pattern among all the T-34 variants of having a great number of interchangeable parts, such as engine, armament, transmission and periscopes. Mechanical simplicity was a prime concern. The hull was of a welded construction throughout and only three different thickness of rolled plate armour were employed.

The suspension was of the Christie pattern, having five large double road wheels on each side with a noticeably larger gap between the second and third wheels. The drive sprocket, located for safety to the rear, was of the roller type used on the BT series and powered a cast manganese-steel track with centre guide horns on alternative track links. This first model of the T-34 had a distinctive turret overhang and a clumsy turret hatch occupying the entire rear part of the turret; it was heavy to lift and blocked the commander's view when the hatch was open. The Model 40 had one periscope fitted on the front left-hand side. In late 1941, a small number of Model 40s were fitted with the long-barrelled, high-velocity 57mm ZIS-4 gun, intended to engage light armoured vehicles at greater ranges than the short 76.2mm L-11 gun.

T-34 (MODEL 1941) (BRITISH CLASSIFICATION 'B')

The second model of the T-34 appeared in 1941 and was essentially a commander's Model 40 with a rolled plate turret mounting a more powerful Model 1940 76.2mm L/41.5 gun. The same clumsy turret hatch was retained, but some of these variants had twin periscopes. While there was no

Above: A late model T-34/85 in the service of the East German Army. The hatch and the cupola of the commander are clearly visible in this picture taken in East Berlin.

change in the layout of the hull, these commanders' tanks had a stowage box on the right-hand track guard. The most noticeable feature of the 1941 model was the replacement of the peculiar cast gun cradle by a new angular bolted type. During 1942 a model appeared with a cast turret and this model also had new, wider tracks. Some of these tanks were fitted with a flame-thrower (ATO-41) and had an armoured fuel container on the rear plate of the hull (for the flame-thrower variant see below).

T-34 (MODEL 1942) (BRITISH CLASSIFICATION 'C')

In 1942 the cast turret (as opposed to rolled plate) became standard in the Model 1942. The new turret weighed 4.4 tonnes (4.32 tons) and had a ring diameter of 1.38m (4.6ft). The Model 1942 had various improvements taking account of the reports reaching the T-34 design teams from the battlefield. The large clumsy hatch, so evident on the earlier models, was replaced by two separate hatches for the commander and gunner. There was also a new hull machine-gun mounting to make the 7.62mm Degtaryev DT machine-gun more effective in close-quarter battle.

In early 1942 a team designed a new T-34, the T-34M, with a chassis similar to the KV tank (with smaller road wheels), and a completely new hull and turret layout. However, this tank was not accepted for production and only the hexagonal shape to the T-34/M turret was retained for the next variant of the T-34, the T-34/76 Model 1943.

The T-34 Model 1943 was manufactured in response to battlefield reports which showed that one serious drawback of the current T-34 design was the turret overhang at the rear of the T-34. It had become accepted practice for German infantry to climb on to the back of T-34s and wedge a Teller mine under the rear of the turret. The overhang had the effect of creating a shot trap that deflected the force of the explosion of the mine into the turret ring, rather than away from the tank. The remedy was a new, cast hexagonal turret with no overhang that became the Model 1943. The T-34 evolved with the experience of battle and the T-34 Model 1943 also included other changes such as improved fuel capacity and welded armour plate components.

T-34/76E

Subsequent T-34/76 models are best known by their British classification as the Soviets did not recognise them as different models marked out by their year of production. The Models 'E' and 'F' were both produced in 1943. While the basic hull and turret structure of the 1943 Model 'E' remained the same, this model incorporated a more effective

Below: Front view of a Yugoslav Army T-34/85 in Belgrade. A machine gun next to the commander's hatch for anti-aircraft and anti-personnel use is clearly visible.

air cleaning and lubrication system. In this model, the hull design was also improved by using automatic welding processes with improved materials that gave higher quality joins and so better resistance to incoming fire. The Model 'E' showed the advances in Soviet industry which fed down the line to the equipment that the Soviet forces used. A new confidence in tank construction that built upon the T-34's obvious successes meant that each new T-34 model was better equipped and more able to withstand the rigours of the battlefield.

T-34/76F

The model 'F' had a distinctive appearance as, while it had no commander's cupola, the model had contoured undercuts around all the sides and the front. The main difference to the 'F' was, however, in its internal workings rather than its external appearance. The T-34/76F had new highly efficient automotive components. The old four-speed gearbox was replaced by a five-speed box that made gear changing easier and increased the speed of the T-34. The air filter was refined further and a level of care and thought went into the mechanics of the T-34/76F that set it apart from earlier

T-34 variants

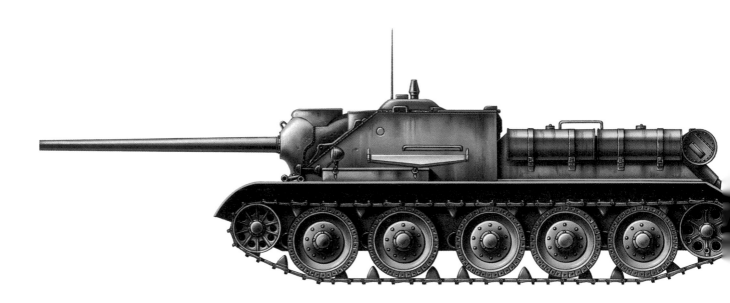

Above: An SU-85 of the 1st Czechoslovak Tank Brigade, summer 1944. The SU-85 was first used in the late summer of 1943, and quickly proved itself capable of knocking out the German Panther.

Below: The PT-34 mine-clearer, which was used on a large scale for the first time during Operation 'Bagration' in the summer of 1944. This vehicle belongs to the 116th Separate Engineer Tank Regiment.

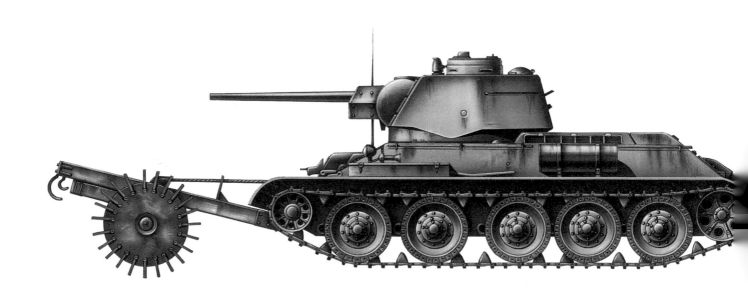

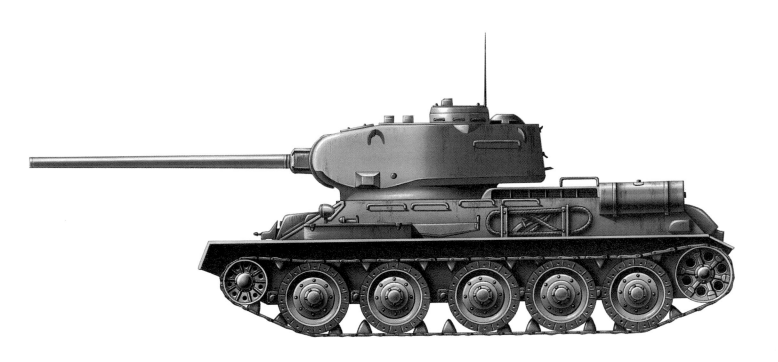

Above: A T-34/85 of the Egyptian 4th Armoured Division in June 1967. This unit fought the Israelis in the 1967 Arab–Isreali War, and suffered heavy losses.

Below: Modified T-34 flamethrower tanks were designated OT-34. The Red Army used flamethrowers mainly for offensive operations against entrenched infantry.

Above: A captured SU-85 tank destoyer with German markings is directed into a tank depot. Germany used captured Soviet armour as her economy was unable to turn out sufficient tanks for the front.

models. However, only a limited number of this type were produced as production moved in a more radical direction.

By 1943 it was apparent that the 76.2mm gun on the T-34 was inadequate. The T-43 model incorporated many new design features, and had added armour protection, but was still undergunned. The appearance of the German long-barrelled 75mm (L/48) and 88mm tank guns firing high-velocity projectiles proved that the Russians had to up-gun the T-34. This led to the genesis of the T-34/85.

T-34/85-I

Towards the end of 1943 the new up-gunned T-34 was complete. With its 85mm gun, the T-34/85-I was basically an up-gunned T-43. The T-34/85 had a new turret originally designed for the KV-85 tank with a ring diameter of 1.56m (5.2ft). This created the space for an extra crew member and simplified the tasks of the tank commander who previously had helped with the gun. The T-34/85-I was first issued to élite Guards Tank units and the new gun soon proved its worth. Based upon the pre-war M-1939 85mm anti-aircraft gun (the German 88mm was also originally an anti-aircraft gun), the T-34/85's gun had an effective range of 1000m (1100yds) and, it was claimed, was able to penetrate the frontal armour of the German Tigers and Panthers. In 1944 production of the new T-34/85 outstripped that of the Panther. After the war was over, the Soviets improved upon the T-34/85-I with a new model known as the T/34-85-II. First introduced in 1947, this was basically the same as the earlier model but with improvements in transmission and armour design and more sophisticated vision and fire-control instruments. This was the model that was extensively employed by the North Koreans in the Korean War, 1950–53, where some of the tanks were also fitted with muzzle brakes. The value of this model is shown by the fact that the Russians continued

production long after the Korean War was over, only ceasing in 1964 by which time some 12,000 models had rolled off the production lines.

T-44

In 1944, as the Soviet forces pushed into Poland, a new medium tank was built that was based on the T-34/85. This armoured fighting vehicle was named the T-44 but due to the pressure of the war it was never allowed to develop into a fully fledged combat vehicle. The T-44 was a 35.7-tonne (35-ton) tank mounting an 85mm gun and saw some action against the Germans in 1945. It was also used in the suppression of the Hungarian uprising in 1956 and continued as a training vehicle into the 1960s. The T-44 had a lower silhouette and a new transversely mounted transmission system. This model was produced in three factories but production ended in 1949 and it was only issued in limited numbers and never to Soviet satellite countries. It was the first tank that had a transversely mounted engine and torsion-bar suspension. By dispensing with the hull machine-gunner, the T-44 had a crew of four, and this allowed more convenient stowage of ammunition. The turret of the T-44 was larger and more heavily sloped compared to the T-34. The T-44 spanned the gap between the T-34 and the later generation of post-war Soviet tanks that began with the T-54. The hull, with its welded construction, was the model for the T-54. The driver's hatch was moved to the top of the hull (from the glacis plate) and this strengthened the glacis plate. Features such as this were also carried over into the T-54. Some T-44s were fitted with a 100mm gun, but with production of the T-54 from 1947, which incorporated many of the features of the T-44, the T-44 was rendered obsolete.

OT-34 FLAMETHROWER

Soviet tank flamethrowers before 1941 were based on the T-26 light tank chassis. The destruction of Soviet tanks in 1941 following Barbarossa was such that the Soviet army needed a new tank flamethrower. Therefore, Russian teams added a flamethrower unit (the ATO-41) to the T-34 to make the first T-34 flamethrower variant. The ATO-41 could also be mounted in the heavier KV tank. The flamethrowers were mounted in place of the usual DT machine-gun on the right of the hull glacis and with 100 litres (22 gallons) of fuel could fire three bursts in 10 seconds. The range was 46–82m (50–90yds) depending on the type of fuel used.

Later in the war, the Russians developed more sophisticated flamethrowers, but still kept the T-34's main armament even when in a flamethrower role. In 1943, under the Allied Aid Agreement, a unit of British flamethrowing Churchill 'Crocodiles' was shipped to Russia from the Petroleum Warfare Department at Langhurst for Russian training. Consequently, the Soviets revamped their T-34 flamethrower and redesignated the flamethrower the ATO-42. The actual tanks equipped with the flamethrower were designated OT-34s (Ogniemetnyi Tank 34, sometimes also called the TO-34) and first employed in 1944. The OT-34 carried 200 litres (44 gallons) of fuel and was operated by compressed air. The OT-34 could achieve a range of 75-90m (82-98yds) with unthickened fuel, or up to 109m (120yds) with thickened fuel. The actual flame gun was mounted in an armoured casting on the right-hand side of the T-34's glacis and had five degrees of traverse either side. Operation was by electric pump and started by firing a 20mm cartridge. Six shots could be fired, each of about two seconds' duration, with the whole operation, including the fuel for the flame ,stored within the tank. Some experimental models of the OT-34 are believed to have been equipped with dual flame guns on the glacis, one on each side of the driver. Because of the amount of flamethrower equipment, the OT-34's radio had to be moved into the rear turret bustle giving the OT-34 a distinctive appearance.

Organisation of the flamethrowing tanks at the front was typically in battalion formation with two companies of KV-8 heavy flamethrowers with 10 tanks, and one company of 11 OT-34 medium flamethrowers. As the KV-8 became more scarce in 1943, the flamethrower battalions were reorganised with two companies of OT-34s supported by a company of standard T-34s for fire support. The OT-34 was primarily used in an offensive role against entrenched German positions, particularly as it was felt that the use of flamethrowers demoralised German infantry defending those positions. The small fuel reservoirs on the OT-34 limited their effectiveness as they were only capable of about 10 flamethrowing bursts.

PT-34 MINECLEARER

The starting point for Soviet mine-clearing tanks was the pre-war PT-3 mineroller. Developed at the Dormashina plant, the PT-3 comprised two sets of steel rollers attached to the tank on a swivelling girder system. By May 1942, a Russian designer, Pavel Mugalev, had adapted the pre-war PT-3 following tests of prototypes at the NKPS plant in Tula for use on the T-34. Two types of mineclearer evolved for the T-34: one had a single axle with 'A' shaped beaters attached to the rims of the discs; the other had a split axle. The first test for the new mineroller, designated the PT-34 (PT standing for Protivotankoviy), came in August 1942. At fighting near Voronezh, PT-34 minerollers with the 223rd Tank Battalion of the 86th Tank Brigade used two of the experimental PT-34s to beat through German minefields. The PT-34 was also used in the battle for Stalingrad, most famously in the assault by the 16th Guards Tank Battalion on the Kanteirovets airfield in the Russian 'Uranus' counter-attack that encircled Stalingrad. These early mineclearers had many teething problems and not until the summer of 1943 were the T-34 mineclearers

Below: A T-34 Tank Recovery Vehicle equipped with a snorkel for water operations. These vehicles were fitted with winches, push-bars and other features, as well as heavy duty cranes.

Above: When the T-34's turret was removed the vehicle could be configured for a number of engineer roles. This is the bridge layer equipped with a scissors-type bridge.

deployed in any number. To make the PT-34 effective, regular engineer tank units were developed to use the mineclearers. The first of these was the 166th Separate Engineer Tank Regiment which was used at the battle of Kursk (where extensive minefields were laid by both sides) for special break-through operations. The 166th Regiment had 22 T-34s and 18 sets of PT-34 minerollers. At the same time as the PT-34 was being deployed, tests were being conducted on 'Lend-Lease' Shermans and Churchills.

The PT-34 was able to withstand a maximum of 10 detonations of 5–10kg (11–22lb) anti-tank mines, after which the rollers had to be replaced. It was a big improvement on the usual tactic of sending forward standard T-34s to clear the minefields unaided when the tank crew had to hope their tank could withstand the force of any explosions. In the Soviet 'Bagration' offensive of the summer of 1944, the Russians first used PT-34s on a wide scale to destroy German Army Group Centre. At least five OT-34 regiments were employed: the 148th and 253rd with the 3rd Byelorussian Front, the 40th with the 3rd Shock Army, and the 119th and 166th PT-34 regiments with the 1st Byelorussian Front. During the Vistula-Oder Offensive, two regiments, the 92nd and 116th, were deployed with the advancing Soviet forces. The PT-34 design, based on the PT-3 mineroller, was the basis for today's modern Russian mineroller systems, and the American mineroller system in use on the M1A1 Abrams

Main Battle Tank in Operation 'Desert Storm' also derived from the earlier Russian PT-34 system first deployed in 1942.

SU-85 AND SU-100 TANK DESTROYERS

The arrival of the first German Tigers on the Eastern Front in 1943 caused the Soviet High Command to rethink their tank organisations. Examination of a Tiger captured on the Leningrad Front in early 1943 showed that the existing F-34 and ZIS-5 guns on the T-34 and KV heavy tank were no match for the new German tank. Consequently, a crash programme was launched to produce a tank destroyer to take on the Tiger. Trials on captured Tigers proved that the only guns that could penetrate the Tiger's armour were the 85mm anti-aircraft gun and the 122mm A-19 corps gun. Under the leadership of General F.F. Petrov, the design bureau struggled to produce an armoured vehicle on which the 85mm gun could be mounted. The resulting gun (designated the D-5S-85) was mounted on a modified T-34 chassis by a team of engineers led by L. Gorlitskiy at the Uralmash tank plant. The 85mm gun was effective, but the gun mounting (derived from the SU-122) was not so successful. Eventually, a new direct-fire telescopic sight (the TSh-15) with a modified ball mounting was built into the SU-85 and the superstructure of the tank destroyer redesigned. The SU-85 could carry 49 rounds of ammunition and was ready for production in August 1943.

The SU-85s were deployed in two discrete formations. Firstly, there were separate self-propelled battalions equipped with 12 SU-85s and assigned to corps and army command for specialist missions. Secondly, there were larger regiments with four batteries of 16 SU-85s in total and an accompanying T-34 command tank. The aim of the SU-85 was to knock out heavy German tanks; they were not intended for use close to enemy infantry. This meant they lacked a self-defence machine-gun and so, like the German Ferdinand/Elephant fixed turret tank destroyers, were vulnerable in any close-quarter battle. The SU-85's job was to use its powerful gun at stand-off ranges against German armoured vehicles and bunkers.

The SU-85s were first used along the Dnepr River in August 1943 and the tank proved popular as it was one of the few available tanks able to fight German Tigers and Panthers. However, the decision to fit an 85mm gun to the T-34 meant that the SU-85 needed to be up-gunned if it were to continue in service. Therefore, a 100mm gun was fitted to make the SU-100, an even more powerful tank destroyer. As a consequence, production of the SU-85 was halted in September 1944 in favour of the SU-100. In total around 2000 SU-85s were built for the Red Army.

SU-122 ASSAULT GUN

The Soviet SU-122 was a response to the success of the German Sturmgeschutz assault gun. As the assault gun (like the SU tank-destroyer series) had no turret, it was far easier and cheaper to produce. Without the complexities of a turret, assault guns could mount heavier weapons. In April 1942, the Main Artillery Directorate issued an order for an assault gun to several of its tank design teams under the overall direction of the People's Commissariat for the Tank Industry. A number of different prototypes with different gun-calibres and different chassis were developed but none was deemed successful. A design team under G.I. Kashtanov even made a prototype assault gun on a captured German Panzer Mark III. Undeterred, the Soviet High Command ordered fresh trials in October 1942, this time using the chassis of the T-34. The task was passed on to the Uralmash tank plant and the design team was led by L. Gorlitskiy and E. Silnishchikov. The team mounted a standard M-30 Model 1938 122mm howitzer in fully enclosed casement on a modified Model 1943 T-34 hull. The gun was able to elevate from -3 degrees to +26 degrees, and could be traversed 10 degrees either side. The prototype had storage for 40 tank rounds. The success of the tank at trials led to the tank being designated the SU-122 and production began in late 1942. In December 1942, the first self-propelled SU-122 regiments were formed consisting of four batteries of lighter SU-76 assault guns (17 vehicles) and two batteries of the heavier

SU-122s (eight vehicles). In early 1943, the SU-122 saw its first action on the Leningrad Front. The combination of the SU-76 with the SU-122 was not always ideal as the SU-76 had many teething problems. Eventually the SU-122 was organised in separate units. With the new BP-460A shaped-charge anti-tank round, it was a powerful infantry-support weapon, able to tackle enemy strongpoints and tanks at distance. In total, some 1100 SU-122 assault guns were built for use on the Eastern Front. The SU-122 proved the versatility of the T-34 hull on which the 122mm gun was mounted. It was in service with the Soviet Army after the war, was exported abroad, and was used after the war in Africa and Asia.

With the turret removed, the T-34 chassis also provided valuable service as both a towing and repair vehicle. Fitted with a boom, the T-34 chassis acted as an armoured mobile crane and workshop. All vehicles of this type were fitted with earth anchors and winches to allow them to recover and fix broken down or knocked-out Russian tanks. Such ARVs were designated TT-34. After the war, when many T-34s were being replaced with more modern tanks such as the T-54, the Russians turned many of their surplus T-34s into recovery vehicles. In 1958 a programme was launched to convert the remaining T-34s: the turret was removed and a tool platform was added over the engine deck. In addition, large stowing boxes were added to the side of the tank as well as a basic 3.1-tonne (3-ton) crane. IR night vision equipment was also a standard extra. Local depots would customise these ARVs with added winches and pushbars. A limited number of T-34s were converted to heavy crane duties (SPK-5) in 1955. Finally, some SU-85 were converted to ARV and in 1990 some were still in service with the East German Army.

BRIDGE-LAYING

There have been three distinct versions of the T-34 in the bridge-laying role. The first was a rigid 'ARK' type, the second a model with a rigid bridge launched by pivoting about a roller at the front (designated T-34/MTU), and the third was a design employed by the Czechs. The ARK model involved fitting an adjustable platform instead of the T-34 turret. The bridge could not be removed from the tank and the aim was to drive the T-34 into the trench to be bridged and the bridge then adjusted to form a platform across the trench. The rather basic ARK design was supplanted by the second design that could span some 11.25m (37.5ft) and carry loads up to 40.4 tonnes (40 tons). Meanwhile, the Czechs kept the T-34 turret as a house for the bridge-actuating motor and this allowed the extension of a hydraulically operated scissors-type bridge some 19.5m (65ft) in length. This bridge could take weights of up to 35.4 tonnes (35 tons).

Most T-34 models were equipped with either a manually or hydraulically operated dozer blade for general engineer work in clearing mines, snow or earth. In this role, the T-34 still retained its main and secondary armaments. Such tanks were given the designation T-34/STU.

T-34/76 Model 1942 – Specification

Crew	Four
Hull length	6.09m (20ft)
Length, gun forward	6.58m (21.6ft)
Width, tracks	2.98m (9.8ft)
Height	2.57m (8.45ft)
Combat weight	31.39 tonnes (30.9 tons)
Ground pressure	0.64kg sq cm (10psi)
Ground clearance	0.38m (1.25ft)
Fording depth	1.31m (4.3ft)
Maximum gradient	30 per cent
Maximum trench crossing	2.5m (8.2ft)

Suspension type	Christie
Number of roadwheels	Five per side
Tyres	Rubber (sometimes steel)

Powerplant type	V-2-34 diesel engine
Configuration	Four-stroke V-12
Valves	Two per cylinder
Material	Aluminium
Nominal output	500hp @ 1800rpm
Power/weight ratio (combat)	16.2hp/tonne
Capacity	38.9 litres (10.2 US gallons/ 8.6 Imp gallons)
Compression ratio	15:1
Coolant	Water, fan-assisted
Fuel capacity	673 litres (177 US gallons/ 148 Imp gallons)
Additional fuel	Two 45-litre (11.8-Us gallon/ 10-Imp gallon) fuel tanks
Nominal range, road	432km (270 miles)
Nominal range, cross-country	368km (230 miles)
Nominal maximum speed	40km/h (25mph)
Cross-country speed	40km/h (25mph)
Transmission type	Dry multi-plate main clutch, mechanical gearbox, Four gears forward, one reverse
Driven sprocket	Rear
Steering type	Clutch and brake
Minimum turning radius	7.625m (25ft)

Main armament	76.2mm L/41.2 F34 rifled gun
Secondary armament	Two 7.62mm Degtaryev DT MGs
Main armament ammunition	77 rounds:
	19 rounds AP
	53 rounds HE
	5 rounds cannister
Secondary armament ammunition	2400 rounds
Other armament	Personal weapons, handguns, 20 hand grenades

Armour	Homogenous steel plate, electro welded
Hull front	47mm (1.85in)
Hull side	45mm (1.77in)
Hull rear	45mm (1.77in)
Hull top	19mm (.75in)
Hull bottom	20mm (.8in)
Turret front	65mm (2.56in)
Turret sides	65mm (2.56in)
Turret rear	47mm (1.85in)
Turret top	19mm (1in)

Turret traverse method	Electrical
Traverse rate	24 degrees per second
Elevation method	Manual
Elevation range	Plus 30 to minus 3 degrees

The T-34's Main Rivals

VEHICLE	PZKPFW PANTHER AUSF. G	PZKPFW VI TIGER	CROMWELL MK V
Crew	Five	Five	Five
Hull length	6.95m (22.75ft)	6.3m (20.66ft)	6.24m (20.47ft)
Length, gun forward	8.85m (29ft)	8.45m (27.7ft)	6.4m (21ft)
Width	3.25m (10.7ft)	3.72m (12.2ft)	3.05m (10ft)
Height (to hatch)	3m (9.85ft)	3m (9.8ft)	2.46m (8ft)
Weight	45.5 tonnes (44.7 tons)	50.5 tonnes (49.7 tons)	27.9 tonnes (27.45 tons)
Ground pressure (kg sq cm)	0.75	1.04	0.95
Fording capacity	1.9m (6.2ft)	1.6m (5.24ft)	0.9/1.22m (2.95/4ft)
Gradient	70 per cent	70 per cent	47 per cent
Trench	2.45m (8ft)	2.5m (8.2ft)	2.3m (7.54ft)
Step	0.9m (2.95ft)	0.8m (2.6ft)	0.9m (2.95ft)
Suspension type	Torsion bars	Torsion bars	Christie/coil springs
Powerplant	HL230 P30 V-12 petrol	HL230 P45 petrol	R-R Meteor V-12 petrol
Output	700hp	700hp	600hp
Power/weight ratio	15.5hp/tonne	12.3hp/tonne	21.5hp/tonne
Capacity	23,095cc	38,900cc	26,900cc
Fuel capacity	730 litres (193 gallons US)	540 litres (142 gallons US)	525 litres (138 gallons US)
Range, road	200km (120 miles)	195km (120 miles)	280km (175 miles)
Range, cross-country	100km (60 miles)	110km (68 miles)	
Nominal maximum speed	55km/h (34.5mph)	45.4kmph (28mph)	62kmph (38.75mph)
Steering type	Single-radius regenerative	Clutches	Regenerative
Turning radius	4.35m (14.3ft)	not known	In place
Main armament	7.5cm L/70 KwK42	8.8cm L/56 KwK36	75mm L36.5 Mk V
Secondary armament	Two 7.92mm MG34 MG	Two 7.92mm MG	Two 7.92mm Besa MG
Main armament ammunition	82 rounds	92 rounds	64 rounds (composite)
Secondary ammunition	4800 rounds	5100 rounds	4952 rounds
Armour	Rolled, welded	Rolled, welded	Rolled, welded/riveted
Hull front	50–80mm (2–3.1in)	100mm (3.94in)	63mm (2.48in)
Hull sides	40–50mm (1.57–2in)	80mm (3.15in)	32mm (1.26in)
Hull rear	40mm (1.57in)	80mm (3.15in)	32mm (1.26in)
Hull top	16mm (.65in)	25mm (0.98in)	20mm (.78in)
Hull bottom	16mm (.65in)	25mm (0.98in)	14mm (.55in)
Turret front	100mm (3.95in)	100mm (3.94in)	76mm (2.3in)
Mantlet	120mm (4.75in)	120mm (4.72in)	–
Turret sides	45mm (1.77in)	80mm (3.15in)	63mm (2.48in)
Turret rear	45mm (1.77in)	80mm (3.15in)	57mm (2.24in)
Turret top	16mm (.65in)	25mm (0.98in)	20mm (.78in)
Turret traverse	Hydraulic/manual	Hydraulic/manual	Hydraulic/manual
Elevation range (degrees)	+20 to -4 degrees	+17 to -6.5 degrees	+20 to -12.5 degrees
Stabilisation	None	None	None

INDEX